HOW TO
DEAL WITH
ANNOYING
PEOPLE

BOB PHILLIPS
KIMBERLY ALYN

HARVEST HOUSE PUBLISHERS
EUGENE, OREGON

Cover by Dugan Design Group, Bloomington, Minnesota

Cover photo © Digital Vision / Getty Images

HOW TO DEAL WITH ANNOYING PEOPLE
Copyright © 2003/2005 by Bob Phillips and Kimberly Alyn
Published 2011 by Harvest House Publishers
Eugene, Oregon 97402
www.harvesthousepublishers.com

ISBN 978-0-7369-2701-7

The Library of Congress has cataloged the edition as follows:

Library of Congress Cataloging-in-Publication Data
Phillips, Bob, 1940–
    How to deal with annoying people / Bob Phillips and Kimberly Alyn.
        p. cm.
    Includes bibliographical references.
    ISBN 978-0-7369-1444-4 (pbk.)
    1. Interpersonal conflict—Religious aspects—Christianity. 2. Conflict management—Religious aspects—Christianity. 3. Interpersonal relations—Religious aspects—Christianity. I. Alyn, Kimberly, 1965– II. Title.
    BV4597.53.C58P49 2005
    158.2—dc22   2004022061

Printed in the United States of America

11 12 13 14 15 16 17 / VP-KB / 10 9 8 7 6 5 4 3 2

Acknowledgments

Thanks to all the annoying people in the world (you know who you are) for providing plenty of great material for a book like this. It could not have been written without you!

This book was made possible by the hand of God working in the lives of both authors. The Lord has continued to lead, bless, and direct the path that has led to this finished product. Praise God for His mighty work!

A Note from the Authors

Writing is like wrestling alligators…it's an exciting and difficult task. Gene Fowler suggests that writing is easy: "All you do is stare at a blank sheet of paper until drops of blood form on your forehead." Red Smith joins in by stating, "There's nothing to writing—all you do is sit down at a typewriter and open a vein." When it comes to two people authoring a book, Evelyn Waugh makes the humorous observation, "Two or more people getting together to write something is like three people getting together to make a baby."

The writing of this book was a joint effort of two friends who have spent many years speaking, teaching, and consulting with various organizations and businesses. We could have chosen to write it entirely in the third person, thus keeping our personalities out of the material and the illustrations. We could have chosen to split up the content, with Bob writing certain chapters and Kim writing others. We could have chosen to write most of the material in third person and occasionally identify certain portions by stating, "This is Bob speaking" or "This is Kim speaking."

For the most part, we decided to write the illustrations in the first person and much of the text in third person. We chose this method because the illustrations actually happened to either Bob or Kim. By changing the names of the people in the illustrations and not identifying who was speaking, we have kept the power of the event while protecting the confidentiality of the individuals.

We felt that a first-person account of a real-life event would be a more powerful form of presentation. It was our hope that this style of writing would keep the flow of thought running smoothly and that the reader would sense the reality of true-life events. You, as the reader, may be more comfortable pretending either Bob or Kim is the only author. If that would be helpful, then please proceed with that concept in mind. We are both in agreement with the thoughts presented and speak with a unified mind.

Bob Phillips and Kimberly Alyn

Contents

PART II:
Conflict Prevention and Resolution

Introduction

*If you have knowledge, let others
light their candles at it.*
—THOMAS FULLER

———

Everywhere you look, conflict abounds: in the workplace, in the personal lives of individuals, and in our churches. Everyone has been annoyed by someone; consequently, everyone has annoyed other people at some point. One of the major causes of conflict lies in the social-style differences that exist between individuals, and the behaviors that are represented by those social styles.

This book is based on the four basic personality styles that date back to Hippocrates (460-370 BC). The social-styles theory has been called different names, but the basic foundation is the same (chapter 17 is dedicated to that very topic—"The Foundational Basis for the Four Social-Styles Concept"). This book is based on the specific social-styles concept developed by Merrill and Reid, as presented in their book *Personal Styles and Effective Performance*. The basic terminology has been retained, as well as the foundational concepts. The observations and research of the authors are also incorporated into the text.

There are other personality studies and social-style concepts that carry tremendous merit and value. However, the Merrill and Reid social-styles evaluation provides a simple, direct, and easily comprehendible method for grasping and applying these concepts. Other writers who have influenced the materials in this book include Dr. O. Hallesby, Dr. Tim LaHaye, David Keirsey, Marilyn Bates, Isabel Briggs-Myers, Dr. Carl Jung, and Raymond Cattell.

The response to social-styles training from seminar attendees and church presentations has been overwhelming. Both authors have been presenting this topic for many years, and both have experienced positive reaction to the social-styles concept. People find it fun, fascinating, and entertaining. Additionally, it is information that can be immediately applied in their lives, and the results are astounding. As individuals learn and apply this information, they are finding it easier to get along with the people who surround them at work, at home, and in the church.

This book was written with the intent of improving your life. As you discover your own social style and the styles of those around you, you will gain a greater sense of awareness with regard to the behavior patterns of people. As a result, you will learn how to adapt in a manner that will increase cohesiveness in your life. May this book be the first step to improving the quality of your relationships and the quality of your life.

PART I

The Four Social Styles of Annoying People

1

Everybody Has Annoying People Problems

Conflict is normal in human relationships.
It arises because we do not understand
the other person's perspective, vision,
decisions, or behaviors.

━━━ッ━━━

I am so sick of Sue coming in late! She always has some lame excuse." Kelly was venting to Pat over a cup of coffee.

"What's even worse," Pat responded, "is that her boss is too lazy and apathetic to do anything about it."

"Yeah, I noticed!" Kelly jumped in and added some more fuel to the fire. "He's been grating on my nerves, too. He acts like he has a phobia when it comes to making decisions."

"No wonder nothing gets done right around here!" Pat was getting fired up, too.

"Well, when you and I rule the world, things are going to change!" Kelly lifted her coffee cup in a gesture of triumph as she clanged it against Pat's cup. They both laughed as they made their way back to their seats.

I was speaking at a corporate training session when I overheard that conversation during a break. It is not an uncommon exchange in the workplace, because everyone has annoying people problems.

When was the last time someone annoyed you? Most likely within the past hour! Different things annoy different people, but everyone gets annoyed. Someone moves too slowly or too quickly, someone is too impatient or too lenient, someone is too loud or too shy...the list goes on and on.

The differences that exist between individuals are usually the basis for misunderstanding, disagreement, and conflict. All too often, we expect other people to think and respond as we do. We do not give consideration to their specific social style or personality. If we make quick decisions and can juggle five things at once, we expect them to do the same. If we are prompt and always on time, we assume that other people will also be on time. If we are patient and thoughtful, we become offended by someone who is impatient and less sensitive.

The areas of potential conflict are endless. Until we learn the social styles of people, as well as our own, we will remain in a cycle of frustration, misunderstanding, and conflict.

It is impossible to live without conflict. Getting along with other people takes time and effort. The trail of broken relationships and continual conflict leads to frustration and misunderstandings in regard to behavior. There is good news. There are practical tools available to assist you in your efforts to get along with people. This book will equip you with some of the following important tools:

+ A program for understanding your own social behavior and the social behavior of other people

+ A means for understanding how you perceive other people and how they perceive you

✦ Tools for creating and improving work and personal relationships

✦ Techniques for reducing tension and conflict

✦ Suggested tips for improving your communication skills

✦ Help for increasing your tolerance for those who are different from you

✦ Tools for resolving conflict once it arises

You will never be able to completely avoid conflict when you deal with other people. You can, however, discover why others annoy you and why you annoy them. That is the first step to reducing potential conflict in your life and working your way toward a more peaceful existence.

The basis for getting along with people is found in the words of Jesus Christ. One day a religious leader approached Jesus and asked Him to identify the greatest commandment in the Law. Jesus replied, " 'Love the Lord your God with all your heart and with all your soul and with all your mind.' This is the first and greatest commandment. And the second is like it: 'Love your neighbor as yourself.' All the Law and the Prophets hang on these two commandments" (Matthew 22:37-40).

Jesus commanded that we must love our neighbors as ourselves. But who are my neighbors? My neighbor is anyone other than myself: family members, friends, fellow workers, even strangers. My neighbors include even my enemies. My neighbors are those who rub me the wrong way and make me feel uncomfortable.

Jesus directed that we love our neighbors with the same type of love that we have for ourselves—to the same degree and with the same proportion. To the extent that we guard our own feelings, we should care for the feelings of other people. To the degree that we try to reach our own hopes and dreams, we should help other people to achieve their hopes, dreams, and potential. That is not an easy assignment, especially since we often find it difficult to fulfill our own goals.

It is one thing to talk about loving my neighbor, but it is another thing to actually do it. When my neighbor is nice to me, it is easier to love him. But when he is impatient, angry, grumpy, or aloof, loving him becomes difficult. And getting along with my neighbor is even more difficult when I am not getting along with myself. Have you ever been dismayed or disappointed with your own behavior? Have you ever asked yourself, "Why did I do that?" Have you put your foot in your mouth so often that you had to learn to whistle through your toes? Loving ourselves and our neighbors would be so much easier if we understood ourselves and our neighbors better.

The process of understanding our behavior and the behavior of others is difficult, time-consuming, and often draining. It is a struggle we will all face on a continual basis until we meet our Creator. But there is good news: There are workable methods for understanding behavior and improving relationships. It is entirely possible to begin to fulfill Christ's command and truly love our neighbors as ourselves.

As you make your way through this book, you will discover that there are four basic social styles that constitute "annoying people." And you will be one of them! As you discover your own style, you will discover the differences and commonalities you share with some of the other styles. You will discover ways to predict behavior in other people and yourself, and learn to adapt your own behavior to get along better with other people. This process will pave the way to conflict prevention.

2

What Annoys Us About Others

He who loves a quarrel loves sin;
he who builds a high gate invites destruction.
—PROVERBS 17:19

Randy just rolls over everyone and could care less what they think about it." John was a fire captain venting his frustrations in a conflict-prevention-and-resolution training class.

"Now that he's a battalion chief, he thinks he doesn't have to be nice to anyone," another captain joined in.

"He just blurts out whatever comes to mind, and usually at inappropriate times. It's just very annoying!" John was not finished venting.

Another captain in the class came to Randy's defense. "Hey, come on. He's just trying to do his job. That's just how he is."

Someone in the back of the class made a long kissing sound with his hand to his mouth and proceeded to call Randy's defender a "kiss-up." "You're as annoying as he is!" Everyone began to laugh as I shook my head and got them back on track.

First thing Monday morning, Carl was called into the general manager's office. "Carl, I understand that there are some problems in your department," Mr. Martin began.

"What do you mean, sir?" Carl inquired.

"I hear from the other employees that you are hard to work for. They say that when you come around, you never say anything positive. You just seem to give orders in a matter-of-fact, non-caring way. They feel like you are treating them like machines instead of people."

Carl seemed to be shocked by Mr. Martin's comments. Carl had recently been appointed head of the production department, replacing Joe Swift. Joe was a disorganized, backslapping kind of leader. He spent most of his time—and the employees' time—just talking. Production was low under Joe's leadership, and Carl was determined to change the department's image. He wanted the company to get a full day's work from every employee. Carl feared that if he got too close to his fellow workers, he would end up like Joe. So he determined to maintain a businesslike posture. Carl wanted to do his best. He wanted the manager to be proud of him. Now he was being called on the carpet for trying to do a good job. He was confused, disappointed, and angry at the turn of events.

Misunderstanding the Real You

Like Randy and Carl, each of us has been misunderstood. We have all said or done something with pure motives and good intentions that was misinterpreted. We become hurt when people do not understand or accept our comments and actions as we intended them. Misunderstandings between people are one of the main reasons we have trouble getting along with the annoying people in our lives. Like in the scenarios with Randy and Carl, other people have annoyed us in much the same way.

These common experiences lead us to a question. Which is more important in social interaction and interpersonal relationships: the actual behavior or the motivation behind the behavior? Many would say that the motive and intent are more important because the motive causes the behavior. Other people say that actions are more important, contending that no one can see another's motives. No one knows what another person's true intent is. We can only observe what other people say and do.

I tend to agree with the latter position. This is not to say that motives for actions are not important. They are. The problem is that we can only guess another person's motives. Sometimes we guess correctly, but most of the time we do not.

Who, then, is the real you? Is the real you made up of motives and intentions or actions and behaviors? In the eyes of others, the real you is made up solely of what you say and do. No matter how important your motives are, people read you by what they see and hear, not by what you want them to see and hear. That is why this book focuses on our behavior—not our motives—and how our behavior affects other people.

> *The actions of men are the best interpreters of their thoughts.*
>
> —JOHN LOCKE

The problem of interpersonal conflict is one of viewpoint. Our actions are very logical and rational to *us*. They make perfect sense in our mind. Since we know the motivation for our behavior (sometimes), we falsely assume that other people also know the reasons behind our actions. We seem to forget that other people are not always aware of our intentions, as plain as those intentions may seem to us. People around us will often view our actions quite differently than we do because they cannot see our motives. In the minds of other people, your behavior—positive or negative—equals the real you. A business associate shared a story with me that reveals the dangers of interpreting the motives of other people:

> Back in the days when an ice-cream sundae cost much less, a ten-year-old boy entered a hotel coffee shop and sat at a table. A waitress put a glass of water in front of him. He hesitated for a moment, and then looked up at her and asked his question. "How much is an ice-cream sundae?"
>
> "Fifty cents," replied the waitress. The little boy pulled his hand out of his pocket and studied a number of coins in it.
>
> "How much is a dish of just plain ice cream?" he inquired. Some people were now waiting for a table, and the waitress was becoming impatient. She assumed he was just being an annoying ten-year-old.
>
> "Thirty-five cents," she said abruptly. The little boy again counted the coins.
>
> "I'll have the plain ice cream," he said.
>
> The waitress brought the ice cream, put the bill on the table, and walked away. The boy finished the ice cream, paid the cashier, and departed. When the waitress came back, she began wiping down the table and then swallowed hard at what she saw. There, placed neatly beside the empty dish, were two nickels and five pennies—her tip.

It is not at all uncommon for us to assume the motives behind the behavior of other people. If we took the time to really find out what those motives were, we would have less misunderstanding to deal with. If we bypassed many of our assumptions altogether, we would have less conflict to overcome.

We all tend to listen to people and watch their behavior half-heartedly. We move quickly from a casual observation of their behavior to a subjective interpretation and judgment. Many times these hasty judgments can result in emotional turmoil and relationship conflicts.

A man and his four-year-old son boarded a train, and the man seated himself next to the window as the train pulled out of the station. As the man stared quietly out the window, his son became restless. The boy began to wander up and down the aisle. Soon he was climbing on the empty seats, yelling and singing loudly, bothering the other passengers. All the while, his father sat motionless, staring out the window.

An elderly woman had been observing all of this and was fuming inside. *This man probably never disciplines his son! He doesn't even care if he runs wild. I can't believe he's just sitting there daydreaming while his son terrorizes the rest of us.* She could not tolerate the annoyance any longer. She got up from her seat and approached the man. Her angry words stirred him from his deep thought.

"Sir, you should be ashamed of yourself," she began indignantly. "Your son is running loose on this train and bothering everyone. You should control him better."

"I'm sorry. I'll go get him," the man replied. "I wasn't paying attention to him. I was thinking about my wife. She died yesterday, and we are bringing her body home on the train."

No doubt the woman felt foolish and embarrassed when she discovered that her hasty judgment of the man's motives was wrong. Subjective labeling and judgment leads to unnecessary conflict and emotional turmoil. Learning to respond objectively to behavior will pave the way to cohesive relationships.

The more we become aware of the behavior of other people and ourselves, the more we will be able to control our responses. Learning to control our responses and reactions in our work and personal relationships will reduce tension and keep us from annoying each other so much.

Behavior Speaks Louder than Words

Since we are going to focus on behavior, it might be helpful to explain the term. Behavior includes what we say, how we say it, and all our accompanying actions. Of these three elements of behavior, the most powerful communicator is nonverbal behavior, our actions (55 percent). This is commonly called body language. It includes facial expressions, arm and body movement, and body position. Next in line is tone of voice (38 percent). This involves how we say things. And the least powerful element is our spoken message, the actual words (7 percent). Notice how the Total Behavior diagram in chart 2-A illustrates the proportional break-down.

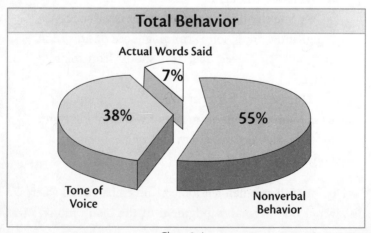

Total Behavior

Actual Words Said

7%

38%

55%

Tone of Voice

Nonverbal Behavior

Chart 2-A

It is important to learn to listen to what people say, but also to listen to tonal inflection. Where the speaker places his or her emphasis makes all the difference in the world. For example, take the phrase "I love you."

✦ *I* love you. Separating myself from all others.

✦ I *love* you. I love you as compared to simply liking you.

✦ I love *you*. Singling you out from everyone else.

✦ I love *you?* Now the tonal inflection goes up at the end of the sentence and forms a question. It says that it is not possible to love you.

Another example of tonal inflection would be in the following sentence: "Bill was caught lying to his supervisor."

Bill	It was Bill, not someone else.
Was	Indicates that the event was in the past, when emphasized.
Caught	Lets you know he was actually caught and not suspected.
Lying	This suggests that this was not Bill's normal behavior when emphasized.
His	Emphasis is on Bill's supervisor versus another supervisor.
Supervisor	Emphasizes that Bill had the nerve to lie to his *supervisor*, and not to just anyone.

If we want to learn to get along with the annoying people in our life, we must become more aware of how people act, rather than what they say or how they say it. Learning how people behave

will help us clearly identify our own behavior. We hope this knowledge will help us become more sensitive and caring toward other
people. Furthermore, becoming aware of how others perceive us
will motivate us to change negative behaviors into positive ones.
Changing behavior will help us build healthy relationships with
our family, friends, and fellow workers.

A Matter of Perspective

Did you hear about the four professors who went on a jungle
safari? They got lost. They had no idea where they were or how to
return to the campsite. You might think that four learned men
could solve such a problem. But these four men could not because
they were blind.

The professors were holding hands and slowly walking along
when they bumped into something. The four men had just found
an old, docile elephant leisurely munching on some grass. The
first professor reached out his hands and grabbed the elephant's
tail. "It feels like some kind of bush," he announced.

The second man bumped his nose on the elephant's side. "It
feels like a wall to me," he said.

The third professor wrapped his arms around the elephant's
front leg. "No, I think you're both wrong," he argued. "It must be
a tree trunk."

The last man groped in the air and his hands touched the elephant's trunk, which quickly encircled the professor's arm.
"Egads!" he cried. "I've grabbed a snake!"

When trying to understand people, we always run the risk of
misunderstanding them. This is because, like the four professors,
we each have a limited personal vantage point. We assess people
from our narrow perspective and hastily slap labels on them. They
can be the labels of personality, culture, religion, vocation, or race.

But like the blind professors, our labels only describe partial truths about people, representing our clouded viewpoints. Our misunderstanding of people, when we mislabel them, is based on incomplete information.

Our descriptions of people basically fall into three areas. First, we describe people based on our view of their actual behavior. For example, we say, "He talks too loudly." "Look how slowly she walks." "His face looks sad, and he speaks softly."

> *Behavior is a mirror in which everyone displays his image.*
> —JOHANN WOLFGANG VON GOETHE

"She looks right at you and stands very rigidly." "He turned his back on me and would not speak."

Second, we describe people based on our thoughts about their inner qualities, traits, characteristics, or motives. We say, "He sure seems ambitious." "She appears interested and sincere." "I think he is a hypocrite." "She is very intelligent and honest."

Third, we describe people based on our emotional reaction to their behavior. We say things like, "He is definitely very strange." "I don't like her." "She really drives me crazy." "I would like to get to know him better." "She seems like a nice person." "I hate him."

Karen didn't take her usual morning coffee break because she was behind in getting the church newsletter edited on her computer. She did not like having a cluttered desk, and she hoped that the extra 15 minutes would help her get her desk cleared. She was intently glued to the monitor to be sure that she would make no errors.

Dave, the senior pastor, noticed Karen working during the coffee break. He thought to himself, *It's so great to have someone in here who is alert and motivated and loves doing the church newsletter.*

Jane, one of the other office employees, turned to Betty and said, "Who does Karen think she is? She's trying to make us look bad for taking a coffee break. She's just trying to impress Dave."

Bill, the youth pastor, walked by Karen's desk and said, "You're sure busy this morning."

Each person had a different interpretation of Karen's actions. Dave evaluated Karen's hard work positively. Jane expressed a negative reaction to her hard work, while Bill simply observed her behavior without judgment.

Subjective and Objective Labels

Descriptions and labels that refer to a person's inner qualities, traits, and characteristics are subjective. So also are the descriptions of our reactions to the behavior of others. Subjectivity is simply the formation of conclusions and mental beliefs without verification. The descriptions by Dave and Jane were subjective. They were based on what they thought or felt Karen was doing. They were both wrong.

Objective description, on the other hand, is based on real facts and observable actions. It is not based on emotion, surmise, or personal prejudice. Bill's observation of Karen's work was objective and correct. She was busy and working hard. Objective description, or labeling, occurs when we talk about a person's actual behavior without trying to apply a reason or motivation for the behavior.

In order to get along with the annoying people in our lives, we need to learn how to observe actual behavior without attempting to judge motives. When we react negatively to a person's behavior or try to subjectively understand someone's motivations, we tend to destroy the possibility of healthy and productive relationships. Dave's description of Karen, though complimentary, was false. What Dave thought was dedicated service was only Karen's obsession with a neat desk. In his subjective description, Dave was setting up Karen and himself for potential future misunderstandings about her work habits.

Labeling people is not bad if our descriptions apply to actual behavior. These kinds of descriptions are not put-downs; they are merely clarifications of actions. We need this kind of labeling. Without it, effective communication would cease. When I walk into the supermarket, I want labels on all the cans and boxes on the shelves. Without labels, grocery shopping and the meals that follow would be a disaster. Similarly, without effective, objective labels for behavior, there will be interpersonal conflict and tension.

Social-style labeling will help us to identify and categorize behavior. As we learn the social styles of other people, we can begin to predict future behavior and adapt to meet their needs. Inevitably, conflict will arise, no matter how familiar we become with each other's social styles. Sometimes minor annoyances escalate into volatile conflict. Part II addresses practical conflict-resolution tools. Regardless of your social style and the social style of other people, there are specific techniques that can be used to resolve conflict before it intensifies.

As you begin to evaluate the information in this book, you will gain a deeper understanding of why you get annoyed by others. You will also begin to see why some of your particular behaviors annoy certain people and not others. Once you are equipped with the knowledge and tools of the four social styles, you will be in a much better position to create harmony in the workplace and at home.

3

Determining
Your Social Style

Nothing in life is to be feared,
it is only to be understood.
—MARIE CURIE

~~~~

Stephen is so uptight about having everything in perfect order. He's driving me nuts! Then when we get in a fight, he just walks out of the room and refuses to talk to me."

"Yeah, well, what are you complaining about? Brian takes the carefree extreme that nothing should matter that much. Who cares if you're late? Who cares if clothes are on the floor? Stephen sounds like a dream! When Brian and I fight, he unloads on me and really lets me know what he thinks. I try to leave the room, and he follows me and keeps on talking!"

I had to chuckle to myself as I sat listening from a distance. I was thinking, *Stephen sounds like an Analytical, and Brian sounds like an Expressive.*

I have heard men doing the same thing. "Cathy is so strict with the kids. She's always focused on what needs to get done and doesn't want to let anyone relax. I keep telling her to lighten up!"

"Sandy just seems to go with the flow all the time. I wish she would take a stand once in a while and stop avoiding conflict everywhere she goes. She lets people walk all over her."

I have heard similar complaints when parents are comparing notes on their kids. "Annie is so disciplined about her homework and never needs to be pushed, but she can be insensitive to everyone. Kelly is the life of the party, but she's always putting things off until the last minute and just wants to socialize all the time."

"Well, Matt and I keep butting heads. He just doesn't have any goals and seems apathetic about everything. He's lazy, and I feel like I have to ride him constantly to get anything done. He is so stubborn!"

I have heard kids who have plenty to say about their parents, too. "Dad expects me to have my life all mapped out with huge goals and aspirations. I'm just not like him. He's so controlling, and I feel like he's smothering me all the time."

"My mom is always following me around the house picking up after me. She expects me to get straight A's and won't let up on me. I feel like I can never meet her expectations."

Everyone has certain areas where they struggle with other people. These areas are often attributable to social-style differences. Each social style places a different emphasis on different areas of importance. This is where priorities come in. Each social style has a general response to conflict and certain behavior traits that can be observed.

There are four basic social styles: Analytical, Driver, Amiable, and Expressive. As you learn to identify these styles, you can predict certain behavior and understand various responses to conflict. The first and most important step in conflict-prevention is identifying your own social style. This section will guide you through that simple process.

Let's begin by determining if you are an asker or a teller. There are two lists in chart 3-A describing the characteristics of an asker and a teller. Which list describes you more: asker or teller? You may find that there are some characteristics in both lists that describe you, but one will usually describe you more than the other. Select either *ask* or *tell* and check the corresponding box after the chart.

Ask Characteristics	Tell Characteristics
☑ Less assertive, more introverted	❑ More assertive, more extroverted
☑ Outward response under stress: flight	❑ Outward response under stress: fight
☑ Driving emotion and motivation under stress: fear	❑ Driving emotion and motivation under stress: anger
☑ Communicates hesitantly	❑ Readily communicative
☑ Lower quantity of talk	❑ Higher quantity of talk
❑ Pace of speech: slower	☑ Pace of speech: faster
☑ Speech volume: soft	❑ Speech volume: louder
☑ Body movements: slow and deliberate	☑ Body movements: fast and rapid
☑ More tentative and less forceful	❑ Less tentative and more forceful
☑ Reserves opinions	❑ Shares opinions easily
☑ Less confrontive	❑ More confrontational
☑ Nonaggressive	❑ More aggressive
☑ Thoughtful decisions	❑ More decisive
☑ Will not pressure people for decisions	❑ Will pressure people for decisions
❑ Patient	☑ Impatient
☑ Not a huge risk-taker	❑ More of a risk-taker
❑ Avoids the use of power if at all possible	☑ Will use personal and positional power
☑ Attentive listener	❑ Has difficulty listening

Merrill and Reid, *Personal Styles and Effective Performance*; Robert Bolton and Dorothy G. Bolton, *Social Style/Management Style* (New York: AMACOM, 1984), adapted.

Chart 3-A

❏ I see myself as more asking.

❏ I see myself as more telling.

Askers are generally more introverted, less aggressive, and less assertive. Tellers are generally more extroverted, more aggressive, and more assertive. While the traits of an asker or teller are neither good nor bad, extremes in either case can cause serious conflict. If askers never share their feelings, they will be rolled over by other people. If tellers do not keep their assertiveness in check, they will overpower those around them. Each of us will display a degree of asking or telling, preferably in a balanced range.

The next step is to determine if you are task-oriented or relationship-oriented. There are two lists in chart 3-B describing the characteristics of a task-oriented individual and a relationship-oriented individual. Which list describes you more: task or relationship? You may find that there are some characteristics in both lists that describe you, but one will usually describe you more than the other. Select either *task* or *relationship* and check the corresponding box after the chart.

❏ I see myself as more task-oriented.

❏ I see myself as more relationship-oriented.

Task-oriented individuals are ruled more by their thinking, with their emotions well under control. Their self-image is developed as a result of the tasks they accomplish. They usually feel their best when they are getting something done, whether at work or at home.

Relationship-oriented individuals are ruled more by their feelings, with more responsive emotions. Their self-image is developed by the acceptance of other people. They feel best when they are involved in positive relationships, whether at work or at home.

Task Characteristics	Relationship Characteristics
❑ Dress: more formal	☑ Dress: more informal
☑ Topics of speech: current issues and tasks at hand	❑ Topics of speech: people, stories, and anecdotes
❑ Body posture: more rigid	☑ Body posture: more relaxed
☑ Facial expressions: more controlled	❑ Facial expressions: more animated
☑ General attitude: more toward the serious side	❑ General attitude: more toward the playful side
☑ More reserved	❑ More outgoing
☑ Controlled and guarded emotions	❑ Free to share emotions
☑ Filled with facts and data	❑ Filled with opinions and stories
☑ Less interested in small talk	❑ More interested in small talk
☑ Decisions are fact-based	❑ Decisions are feeling or gut-based
☑ Disciplined about time	❑ Less disciplined about time
☑ Strict and disciplined about rules	❑ More permissive and lenient about rules
☑ Restrained and guarded when sharing opinions	❑ More impulsive and forceful when sharing opinions
☑ Hard to get to know, keeps distance from people	❑ Easy to get to know, does not keep distance from people
☑ Preoccupied	❑ More carefree

Merrill and Reid, *Personal Styles and Effective Performance;* Robert Bolton and Dorothy G. Bolton, *Social Style/Management Style,* adapted.

Chart 3-B

As with the ask-and-tell traits, neither the task nor relationship trait is better than the other. Each is merely descriptive of two generally different behaviors. Again, either trait taken to an extreme can lead to conflict. If you are overwhelmingly task-focused, other people may not get to know you or like you. An environment of tension, mistrust, and conflict may develop. If you are so involved with people that you do not accomplish any tasks, you will be viewed as flippant, lazy, and shallow. Each of us will display a degree of task or relationship traits, preferably in a balanced range.

At this point you should have selected either *ask* or *tell* and either *task* or *relationship*. Chart 3-C displays the four basic social styles based on the ask/tell and task/relationship concepts.

Ask/Task **ANALYTICAL**	Tell/Task **DRIVER**
Ask/Relationship **AMIABLE**	Tell/Relationship **EXPRESSIVE**

Chart 3-C

If you selected *ask* and *task*, your social style would be *Analytical*. If you selected *tell* and *task*, your social style would be *Driver*. If you selected *ask* and *relationship*, your social style would be *Amiable*. If you selected *tell* and *relationship*, your social style would be *Expressive*. No specific social style is better than any other (although you are most likely thinking that yours rules!). Each style differs in emphasis and priorities.

The next chapter will describe the basic strengths and weakness of each style. As we progress through this book, we will examine how each social style responds under stress, and we will determine where the biggest conflicts exist between the various styles. Additionally, you will discover which social styles you are the most compatible with. Further chapters will reveal the secrets to working with each style, responding to conflict, leading a particular style, following a particular style, and a variety of other insights that will make your life easier.

4

The Strengths of Each Social Style

With different persons, we may be quite different individuals. We cling, however, to the illusion that we remain identical for all persons and every situation.
—LUIGI PIRANDELLO

⟿

Jerry was sharing his thoughts with one of the other managers. "I love how spontaneous and outgoing Josh is. He's fun and full of charisma. He gets people in the team spirit and can really arouse enthusiasm in the organization. I just wish he would show up on time and follow through more on his projects."

Mary was sharing her own experiences with Jerry as they compared notes. "Well, Wendy is just the opposite. She is always early, dependable, and follows through. She is outstanding at planning projects and seeing them to completion. However, she drives people like Josh nuts at times with her negative input. She can spend way too much time planning and not getting enough done."

As you will soon discover, each social style possesses a list of strengths and weaknesses. Some of the strengths of a particular style can serve as a point of annoyance to another style. Some of the weakness of the social styles can be annoying to every style. That is why we end up with four types of annoying people, and that is also why you end up being one of them!

The good news is that there are traits in every style we can admire and appreciate. Additionally, we can each learn what our negative tendencies are and how to display our positive traits more than our negative ones. We can also learn to modify our behavior to get along better with other people.

Each social style has a particular area of specialty, in addition to general strengths and weaknesses. As you become aware of the different styles, you may find some of your traits in another social style besides your primary style. Everyone has a secondary social style in addition to his or her primary style, and we will examine this concept more closely in the next chapter of the book.

Analyticals—The Technique Specialists

Analyticals are precise, and they are experts in the area of technique. Analyticals have a strong sense of duty and obligation. They are driven by a forceful work ethic, and play does not come naturally to them. They are natural givers and often take on the role of parent or guardian for other people and organizations.

Analyticals have a tendency to take on too much responsibility. They see themselves as conservators and tend to worry. They will save and store for the future, believing they cannot save too much. They are steadfast, reliable, and dependable. Listed below are some of the greatest strengths of the Analytical.

Snapshot of the Analytical:

+ Deep and thoughtful
+ Serious and purposeful
+ Genius-prone
+ Talented and creative

- Artistic or musical
- Philosophical and poetic
- Appreciative of beauty
- Sensitive to other people
- Self-sacrificing
- Conscientious
- Idealistic
- Seeks ideal mate

The Analytical at Work:

- Sacrifices own will for other people
- Schedule-oriented
- Encourages scholarship and talent
- Detail-conscious
- Economical
- Perfectionist, high standards
- Persistent and thorough
- Orderly and organized
- Conscientious
- Idealistic
- Neat and tidy
- Sees the problem
- Finds creative solutions
- Likes charts, graphs, figures, and lists
- Finishes what he or she starts

The Analytical as a Parent:

- Sets high standards

✦ Keeps home in good order

✦ Wants everything done right

✦ Picks up after children

The Analytical as a Friend:

✦ Makes friends cautiously

✦ Avoids seeking attention

✦ Content to stay in background

✦ Faithful and devoted

✦ Can solve other people's problems

✦ Will listen to complaints

✦ Deep concern for people

Drivers—The Control Specialists

Drivers are obsessed by a strong compulsion to perform and be in control. They take pleasure in almost any kind of work because it involves activity. Idleness will destroy Drivers. They desire to control and master everything they do. They speak with precision and little redundancy.

Drivers like new ideas, challenges, and competition. They have a passion for knowledge. They are constantly searching to answer the whys of life. They can be overly forceful and may require too much from themselves and other people. Drivers are haunted by the possibility of failure. They are self-controlled, persistent, and logical. Listed below are some of the greatest strengths of the Driver.

Snapshot of the Driver:

✦ Born leader

✦ Dynamic and active

✦ Compulsive need for change

- ✦ Must correct wrongs
- ✦ Strong-willed and decisive
- ✦ Not easily discouraged
- ✦ Unemotional
- ✦ Exudes confidence
- ✦ Can run anything
- ✦ Independent and self-sufficient

The Driver at Work:

- ✦ Goal-oriented
- ✦ Organizes well
- ✦ Sees the whole picture
- ✦ Seeks practical solutions
- ✦ Delegates work
- ✦ Moves quickly to action
- ✦ Insists on production
- ✦ Stimulates activity
- ✦ Thrives on opposition

The Driver as a Parent:

- ✦ Exerts sound leadership
- ✦ Establishes goals
- ✦ Motivates family to action
- ✦ Organizes household
- ✦ Knows the right answers

The Driver as a Friend:

- ✦ Has little need for friends

+ Will work for group activity
+ Will lead and organize
+ Is usually right
+ Excels in emergencies

Amiables—The Support Specialists

Amiables are very likable people who support others. They work well with other people and promote harmony. They are found wrapped up in causes. They like to work with words and often influence large groups through writing. They sometimes place unrealistic expectations on themselves and other people. They will often romanticize experiences and relationships.

Amiables like to have direction. They often observe people and seek deep meaning in relationships and experiences. They prefer interaction to action. Amiables are very compassionate with those who may be hurting. They are patient, good listeners, and are filled with integrity. Listed below are some of the greatest strengths of the Amiable.

Snapshot of the Amiable:

+ Low-key personality
+ Easygoing and relaxed
+ Calm, cool, and collected
+ Patient and well-balanced
+ Consistent life
+ Quiet but witty
+ Sympathetic and kind
+ Keeps emotions hidden
+ Happily reconciled to life
+ All-purpose person

The Amiable at Work:

- ✦ Competent and steady
- ✦ Peaceful and agreeable
- ✦ Has administrative ability
- ✦ Mediates problems
- ✦ Avoids conflict
- ✦ Good under pressure
- ✦ Finds the easy way out

The Amiable as a Parent:

- ✦ Makes a good parent
- ✦ Peaceful and agreeable
- ✦ Not in a hurry
- ✦ Takes time for children
- ✦ Can take the good with the bad

The Amiable as a Friend:

- ✦ Easy to get along with
- ✦ Pleasant and enjoyable
- ✦ Inoffensive
- ✦ Good listener
- ✦ Dry sense of humor
- ✦ Enjoys watching people
- ✦ Has many friends

Expressives—The Social Specialists

Expressives are very impulsive people who love to socialize. They like to try the new and different. They enjoy wandering, and it is easy for them to break social ties. They like to live for the here and now. Expressives struggle with commitment and follow-through.

Expressives have happy and charismatic spirits and can endure hardships and trials easier than the other social styles. Discomfort is just a new experience that they know will pass. They love to reminisce and enjoy belonging to social organizations. They are friendly, giving, and easygoing. Listed below are some of the greatest strengths of the Expressive.

Snapshot of the Expressive:

+ Appealing personality
+ Talkative, storyteller
+ Life of the party
+ Good sense of humor
+ Memory for color
+ Holds on to listeners physically
+ Emotional and demonstrative
+ Enthusiastic and expressive
+ Cheerful and bubbly
+ Curious
+ Good on stage
+ Wide-eyed and innocent
+ Lives in the present
+ Changeable disposition
+ Sincere heart
+ Always a child

The Expressive at Work:

+ Volunteers for jobs

- ✦ Thinks up new activities
- ✦ Looks great on the surface
- ✦ Creative and colorful
- ✦ Has energy and enthusiasm
- ✦ Starts in a flashy way
- ✦ Inspires other people to join
- ✦ Charms people to work

The Expressive as a Parent:

- ✦ Makes home fun
- ✦ Is liked by children's friends
- ✦ Turns disaster into humor
- ✦ Is the ringmaster

The Expressive as a Friend:

- ✦ Makes friends easily
- ✦ Loves people
- ✦ Thrives on compliments
- ✦ Seems excited
- ✦ Envied by other people
- ✦ Does not hold grudges
- ✦ Apologizes quickly
- ✦ Prevents dull moments
- ✦ Likes spontaneous activities

Chart 4-A gives a general overview of each of the styles. Note that each social style has a different and unique way of responding to the specific areas listed on the left-hand side of the chart.

General Overview of the Four Social Styles

Area	Analyticals	Drivers	Amiables	Expressives
Reaction	Slow	Swift	Unhurried	Rapid
Orientation	Thinking and fact	Action and goal	Relationship and peace	Involvement and intuition
Likes	Organization	To be in charge	Close relationships	Much inter-action
Dislikes	Involvement	Inaction	Conflict	To be alone
Maximum effort	To organize	To control	To relate	To involve
Minimum concern	For relationships	For caution in relationships	For effecting change	For routine
Behavior directed toward achievement	Works carefully and alone—primary effort	Works quickly and alone—primary effort	Works slowly and with other people—secondary effort	Works quickly and with teams—secondary effort
Behavior directed toward acceptance	Impresses people with precision and knowledge—secondary effort	Impresses people with individual effort—secondary effort	Gets along as integral member of group—primary effort	Gets along as exciting member of group—primary effort
Actions	Cautious	Decisive	Slow	Impulsive
Skills	Good problem-solving skills	Good administrative skills	Good counseling skills	Good persuasive skills
Decision-making	Avoids risks, based on facts	Takes risks, based on intuition	Avoids risks, based on opinion	Takes risks, based on hunches
Use of time	Slow, deliberate, disciplined	Swift, efficient impatient	Slow, calm, undisciplined	Rapid, quick, undisciplined

Merrill and Reid, *Personal Styles and Effective Performance*; Robert Bolton and Dorothy G. Bolton, *Social Style/Management Style*, adapted.

Chart 4-A

5

The Weaknesses of Each Social Style

The Spirit helps us in our weakness.
—ROMANS 8:26

―――――

Well, look who woke up on the wrong side of the bed! Andy is nitpicking every aspect of that report we did. He is so critical sometimes! You'd think he could just make a decision and get on with it." Amanda was peeking through the blinds at the office across the hall while complaining to Joe.

"Stop spying! He'll see you!" Joe pulled Amanda away from the window. "Look, we did the best we could. Andy will always play the devil's advocate and make sure no stone goes unturned. Personally, I just think he needs to get a life!"

Andy sighed heavily in frustration as he went through the report. *This is not even what I asked for. If Amanda would just slow down and take her time, she would get it right the first time. She is just too eager to get on with the next project to care about this one. I'm always the one stuck cleaning up everyone's messes around here.*

Every social style has its weaknesses. We all display our weakness in different ways. Analytical styles like Andy are very thorough and exacting, but can be viewed by other styles as negative and obsessive. Driver styles like Amanda get things done quickly, but do not like paying attention to detail. As you begin to learn more about your negative tendencies, you can examine ways to change your behavior so you can display more of your positive traits and less of your negative ones. Review the lists below of each social style and its weaknesses.

The Analytical's Weaknesses

Snapshot of the Analytical:

+ Remembers the negative
+ Moody and depressed
+ Enjoys being hurt
+ False humility
+ Off in another world
+ Low self-image
+ Selective hearing
+ Self-centered
+ Too introspective
+ Guilt feelings
+ Persecution complex
+ Tends to hypochondria

The Analytical at Work:

+ Not people-oriented
+ Depressed over imperfections
+ Chooses difficult work

- ✦ Hesitant to start projects
- ✦ Spends too much time planning
- ✦ Prefers analysis to actual work
- ✦ Hard to please
- ✦ Standards often too high
- ✦ Deep need for approval

The Analytical as a Parent:

- ✦ Puts goals beyond reach
- ✦ May discourage children
- ✦ May be too meticulous
- ✦ Becomes a martyr
- ✦ Sulks over disagreements
- ✦ Puts guilt on children

The Analytical as a Friend:

- ✦ Lives through other people
- ✦ Withdrawn and remote
- ✦ Socially insecure
- ✦ Critical of people
- ✦ Holds back affection
- ✦ Dislikes those in opposition
- ✦ Suspicious of people
- ✦ Antagonistic and vengeful
- ✦ Unforgiving
- ✦ Full of contradictions
- ✦ Skeptical of compliments

The Driver's Weaknesses

Snapshot of the Driver:

+ Bossy
+ Impatient
+ Quick-tempered
+ Cannot relax
+ Too impetuous
+ Enjoys controversy and arguments
+ Will not give up when losing
+ Comes on too strong
+ Inflexible
+ Not complimentary
+ Dislikes tears and emotions
+ Is unsympathetic

The Driver at Work:

+ Little tolerance for mistakes
+ Demands loyalty in ranks
+ Does not analyze details
+ Bored by trivia
+ May make rash decisions
+ May be rude or tactless
+ Manipulates people
+ Demanding of people
+ Feels the end justifies the means
+ Work may become God

The Driver as a Parent:

✦ Tends to overdominate

✦ Too busy for family

✦ Gives answers too quickly

✦ Impatient with poor performance

✦ Will not let children relax

✦ May send children into depression

The Driver as a Friend:

✦ Tends to use people

✦ Dominates people

✦ Decides for other people

✦ Knows everything

✦ Can do everything better

✦ Is too independent

✦ Possessive of friends and mate

✦ Cannot say "I'm sorry"

The Amiable's Weaknesses

Snapshot of the Amiable:

✦ Unenthusiastic

✦ Fearful and worried

✦ Indecisive

✦ Avoids responsibility

✦ Quiet will of iron

✦ Selfish

✦ Too shy and reticent

✦ Too compromising
✦ Self-righteous

The Amiable at Work:

✦ Not goal-oriented
✦ Lacks self-motivation
✦ Hard to get moving
✦ Resents being pushed
✦ Lazy and careless
✦ Discourages other people
✦ Would rather watch

The Amiable as a Parent:

✦ Lax on discipline
✦ Does not organize the home
✦ Takes life too easily
✦ Will ignore family conflict

The Amiable as a Friend:

✦ Dampens enthusiasm
✦ Stays uninvolved
✦ Is not exciting
✦ Indifferent to plans
✦ Judges people
✦ Sarcastic and teasing
✦ Resists change

The Expressive's Weaknesses

Snapshot of the Expressive:

+ Compulsive talker
+ Exaggerates and elaborates
+ Dwells on trivia
+ Cannot remember names
+ Scares people off
+ "Too" happy for some people
+ Restless energy
+ Egotistical
+ Blusters and complains
+ Naive and gullible
+ Loud voice and laugh
+ Controlled by circumstances
+ Angers easily
+ Seems phony to some people
+ Never grows up

The Expressive at Work:

+ Would rather talk
+ Forgets obligations
+ Does not follow through
+ Confidence fades fast
+ Undisciplined
+ Priorities out of order

✦ Decides by feelings
✦ Easily distracted
✦ Wastes time talking

The Expressive as a Parent:

✦ Keeps home in a frenzy
✦ Forgets children's appointments
✦ Disorganized
✦ Does not listen to the whole story

The Expressive as a Friend:

✦ Hates to be alone
✦ Needs to be center stage
✦ Wants to be popular
✦ Looks for credit
✦ Dominates conversations
✦ Interrupts and does not listen
✦ Answers for people
✦ Fickle and forgetful
✦ Makes excuses
✦ Repeats stories

Charts 5-A and 5-B give a general overview of the positive and negative traits of each social style. These are useful charts for examining the natural strengths and weaknesses of your social style. Once you become familiar with those, you can start to concentrate on minimizing your weaknesses and maximizing your strengths. Additionally, you can pinpoint the strengths and weaknesses of people with whom you work and live. You can begin to understand why some people annoy you and how to cope with them.

Strengths and Weaknesses of Analyticals and Drivers

Analyticals		Drivers	
Negative	**Positive**	**Negative**	**Positive**
Moody	Industrious	Unsympathetic	Determined
Critical	Gifted	Pushy	Independent
Negative	Perfectionist	Insensitive	Productive
Rigid	Conscientious	Inconsiderate	Strong-willed
Persistent	Loyal	Severe	Visionary
Indecisive	Aesthetic	Hostile	Optimistic
Legalistic	Idealistic	Sarcastic	Active
Self-centered	Exacting	Tough	Practical
Stuffy	Sensitive	Unforgiving	Courageous
Touchy	Self-sacrificing	Domineering	Decisive
Vengeful	Orderly	Opinionated	Self-confident
Picky	Self-disciplined	Prejudiced	Efficient
Unsociable		Harsh	Leader
Moralistic		Proud	

Chart 5-A

Strengths and Weaknesses of Amiables and Expressives

Amiables		Expressives	
Negative	**Positive**	**Negative**	**Positive**
Unbothered	Calm	Weak-willed	Outgoing
Conforming	Supportive	Manipulative	Ambitious
Blasé	Easygoing	Restless	Charismatic
Indolent	Likable	Disorganized	Warm
Unsure	Respectful	Unproductive	Stimulating
Spectator	Diplomatic	Excitable	Responsive
Selfish	Efficient	Undependable	Talkative
Stingy	Willing	Undisciplined	Enthusiastic
Stubborn	Organized	Obnoxious	Carefree
Dependent	Conservative	Loud	Compassionate
Self-protective	Practical	Reactive	Dramatic
Indecisive	Dependable	Exaggerates	Generous
Awkward	Reluctant Leader	Egotistical	Friendly
Fearful	Agreeable		
	Dry humor		

Chart 5-B

6

Secondary Social Styles

Know yourself. Don't accept your dog's admiration
as conclusive evidence that you are wonderful.
—ANN LANDERS

When I teach seminars on the social-styles concept, people quickly discover the concept of secondary social styles. I begin the seminar by having everyone determine his or her own social style. Each person checks off the characteristics that most apply to him or her from the ask/tell list and the task/relationship list. After everyone in the group has established what social style best describes him or her, I break the group into Drivers, Analyticals, Expressives, and Amiables.

Once I have everyone in his or her social-style group, I give each group an interactive remote control to answer the questions that will appear on the screen in front of the room. Each group has to decide among themselves how they will answer the question as a group. Here is an example of a question that they might receive:

In the workplace, I get most irritated by someone who:

A) Makes decisions too quickly

B) Makes decisions too slowly

C) Is too pushy

D) Socializes too much

Each group will tend to answer consistently in accordance with its social style. Most Drivers are irritated by people who make decisions too slowly or people who socialize too much. Analyticals are most irritated by people who make rash decisions or people who are too pushy. Amiables are usually irritated by people who are too pushy. Expressives are most irritated by people who make decisions too slowly.

As the group engages in discussion, it is fascinating to watch the dynamics. The Driver group usually has its answer registered first (the quick decision-makers). Expressives sometimes take a while because they like to talk a lot. Other times, they answer quickly and impulsively. Amiables may take a while because they all want someone else in the group to make the final decision. Analyticals usually answer last because they want to be sure they have thoroughly explored all of the potential options.

As each group begins their discussion, someone in the group may wander outside the "norm." For example, the Driver group may be talking among themselves about how irritating it is to have someone take forever to make a decision. The group seems to be agreeing to select "B) Makes decisions too slowly," when someone speaks up.

"Well, sometimes decisions do need to be thought through more carefully, and I am leaning toward 'C) Is too pushy.'" Although this person is primarily a Driver, this person is displaying a secondary social style (most likely Analytical).

Each social style has a secondary, less-dominant style. Your secondary style is what makes you unique and sets you apart from other people with that same style. Determining your secondary style is similar to determining your primary social style. Let's look at an example.

Linda has gone through the lists of ask and tell characteristics from chart 3-A (in chapter 3). The results of her selections are listed on Chart 6-A.

Ask Characteristics	Tell Characteristics
☐ Less assertive, more introverted	☑ More assertive, more extroverted
☐ Outward response under stress: flight	☑ Outward response under stress: fight
☐ Driving emotion and motivation under stress: fear	☑ Driving emotion and motivation under stress: anger
☐ Communicates hesitantly	☑ Readily communicative
☐ Lower quantity of talk	☑ Higher quantity of talk
☐ Pace of speech: slower	☑ Pace of speech: faster
☐ Speech volume: soft	☑ Speech volume: louder
☐ Body movements: slow and deliberate	☑ Body movements: fast and rapid
☐ More tentative and less forceful	☑ Less tentative and more forceful
☐ Reserves opinions	☑ Shares opinions easily
☐ Less confrontive	☑ More confrontive
☐ Nonaggressive	☑ More aggressive
☐ Thoughtful decisions	☑ More decisive
☐ Will not pressure people for decisions	☑ Will pressure people for decisions
☐ Patient	☑ Impatient
☐ Not a huge risk-taker	☑ More of a risk-taker
☐ Avoids the use of power if at all possible	☑ Will use personal and positional power
☐ Attentive listener	☑ Has difficulty listening

Chart 6-A

❑ I see myself as more asking.

☑ I see myself as more telling.

Linda then took inventory of her task versus relationship characteristics. Her results are shown on chart 6-B.

Task Characteristics	Relationship Characteristics
☑ Dress: more formal	❑ Dress: more informal
☑ Topics of speech: current issues and tasks at hand	❑ Topics of speech: people, stories, and anecdotes
❑ Body posture: more rigid	☑ Body posture: more relaxed
❑ Facial expressions: more controlled	☑ Facial expressions: more animated
❑ General attitude: more toward the serious side	☑ General attitude: more toward the playful side
❑ More reserved	☑ More outgoing
☑ Controlled and guarded emotions	❑ Free to share emotions
☑ Filled with facts and data	☑ Filled with opinions and stories
☑ Less interested in small talk	❑ More interested in small talk
☑ Decisions are fact based	❑ Decisions are feeling- or gut-based
☑ Disciplined about time	❑ Less disciplined about time
☑ Strict and disciplined about rules	❑ More permissive and lenient about rules
☑ Restrained and guarded when sharing opinions	☑ More impulsive and forceful when sharing opinions
☑ Hard to get to know, keeps distance from people	❑ Easy to get to know, does not keep distance from people
☑ Preoccupied	❑ More carefree

Chart 6-B

❏ I see myself as more relationship-oriented.

☑ I see myself as more task-oriented.

After reviewing the lists, Linda could easily see that she was a teller and was predominately task-oriented. She determined that her primary social style was Driver. To determine her secondary style, she reviewed these lists again and realized that she had many of the relationship-oriented traits, but none of the asking traits. So her secondary style would be tell/relationship, which is an Expressive. So her primary style would be Driver and her secondary style would be Expressive, making her an Expressive Driver. The secondary style serves as an adjective to describe the manner in which you conduct your primary style, which is a noun. Linda would be somewhat Expressive in the manner she behaves as a Driver.

Linda also went through the lists of strengths and weaknesses of each style and noticed that the Driver definitely described most of her strengths and weaknesses. The Expressive lists had many characteristics that described her as well, but not as predominately as the Driver characteristics. Since Linda had none of the characteristics described on the ask list, we know that her secondary style would not be an Amiable or an Analytical (both are askers).

Had Linda selected all of the ask characteristics instead of tell characteristics, and her answers remained the same in the category of task/relationship, her primary style would have been Analytical (ask/task). Since she possessed some of the relationship characteristics, her secondary style would have been Amiable (ask/relationship). If she possessed none of the tell characteristics, we know that her secondary style would not have been Driver or Expressive.

When you combine the primary and secondary social styles, you will find 16 possible styles (primary styles are in all caps, and secondary styles are in lowercase). Review chart 6-C for an overview of the primary and secondary social styles.

The 16 Social-Style Combinations:

- ✦ Analytical ANALYTICAL
- ✦ Driver ANALYTICAL
- ✦ Amiable ANALYTICAL
- ✦ Expressive ANALYTICAL

- ✦ Analytical DRIVER
- ✦ Driver DRIVER
- ✦ Amiable DRIVER
- ✦ Expressive DRIVER

- ✦ Analytical AMIABLE
- ✦ Driver AMIABLE
- ✦ Amiable AMIABLE
- ✦ Expressive AMIABLE

- ✦ Analytical EXPRESSIVE
- ✦ Driver EXPRESSIVE
- ✦ Amiable EXPRESSIVE
- ✦ Expressive EXPRESSIVE

Primary and Secondary Styles

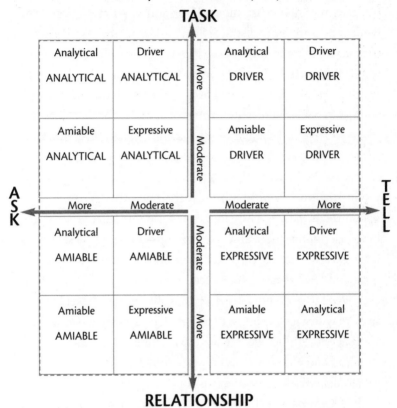

TASK

Analytical ANALYTICAL	Driver ANALYTICAL	Analytical DRIVER	Driver DRIVER
Amiable ANALYTICAL	Expressive ANALYTICAL	Amiable DRIVER	Expressive DRIVER
Analytical AMIABLE	Driver AMIABLE	Analytical EXPRESSIVE	Driver EXPRESSIVE
Amiable AMIABLE	Expressive AMIABLE	Amiable EXPRESSIVE	Analytical EXPRESSIVE

ASK — More | Moderate | Moderate | More — TELL

RELATIONSHIP

Anthony J. Alessandra, *Non-Manipulative Selling* (Reston, VA: Reston Publishing Co., 1981), adapted from p. 24.

Chart 6-C

Once you have determined your primary and secondary social style, you may be wondering how you became an Analytical or a Driver. Maybe you are wondering if you were once an Expressive and now you are an Amiable. The answer is simple: You are born with your basic social style, and you will die with it.

Social styles can be observed in very young children. You will notice some infants are more clingy and relationship-oriented while others are more distracted and task-oriented. As they begin to talk, you can observe very distinct ask and tell characteristics as well. Children are often labeled as "shy," or "outgoing." Most of the descriptions can be traced back to the four basic social styles.

Again, you are born with your social style, but that does not mean you will not change your behavior through the years. Your social style determines what your natural-behavior tendencies are. As people learn what their tendencies are, they learn how to modify their behavior to minimize their negative tendencies and maximize the positive. Amiables may learn through the years how to voice opinions more and take stands on difficult issues. Drivers may learn to modify their behavior and put more priority on people instead of tasks. Analyticals may learn to make decisions even when they do not have every possible fact available. Expressives may learn to modify their behavior and tone down their approach to conflict. People tend to become more aware of their strengths and weaknesses as they grow older and learn to adapt to get along better with people (we hope).

It will always be a challenge for Drivers and Expressives to tone it down and not be so pushy. It will always be a challenge for Analyticals and Amiables to make decisions in a timely manner. Each social style has specific areas that will require more effort than the other social styles. While you may learn how to change your response to certain circumstances and modify your behavior, you will always have the primary and secondary social style you were born with.

You may also be wondering if it is possible to possess traits from the other social styles as well. (If you see yourself as all four social styles, you are most likely an Analytical!) The answer is yes.

However, the percentage of traits from the other social styles diminishes greatly compared to the primary and secondary traits. Using the Driver as the primary style and the Analytical as the secondary, chart 6-D visually depicts this concept.

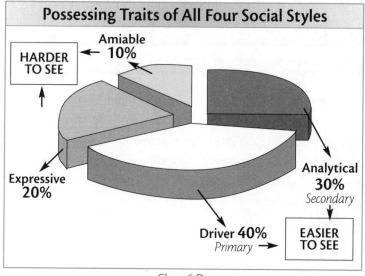

Chart 6-D

There are obviously other factors that create individuality in each person as well. In addition to the primary and secondary social styles, there are other considerations when examining behavior. The environmental upbringing of each person will play a role in his or her individuality and behavioral tendencies. Social and religious influences will factor into the behavior of each person, as well as cultural issues.

Although there are a variety of factors that influence behavior, the study of basic social styles seems to provide the most insight to predicting behavior. Social-style examination can help to explain why some people handle circumstances differently in their lives.

How can two people from the same family go through extreme trauma and one emerges seemingly unscathed, while the other person cannot seem to get over it? Social-style differences provide some insight into this mystery. As you begin to evaluate the responses of each style in regard to stress and other related areas, you begin to see some trends among the different social styles.

In studying the different characters of the Bible, we can observe very distinct social-style behavior. Paul was a Driver, while Moses was an Analytical. Abraham was an Amiable, and Peter was an Expressive. You will find every social-style combination in the Bible.

Each person on earth is very unique and is individual in his or her thinking, behavior, and beliefs. Yet each individual has some very distinct similarities to other people who share his or her social style. All Drivers have certain traits in common, as do Analyticals, Amiables, and Expressives. The uniqueness of each individual is what keeps life interesting!

7

The Annoying People in Action

You can observe a lot just by watching.
—YOGI BERRA

⎯⎯⎯⎯⎯

Becoming very impatient with Ron's driving, Amy said, "Do you have *any* idea where you're going?"

"Calm down. Of course I do. Why are you so impatient?" Ron glanced down at the map in his lap.

"Maybe it has something to do with how *slow* you drive! Don't you notice everyone riding your bumper and flying past you at top speed?"

"Who cares? I'm not going to drive like a maniac just to appease other drivers." Ron began to slow down even more as he looked for the street he wanted to turn down.

Clint put in his two cents from the backseat. "*Whoa!* Did you see that guy give you the finger? Speed it up, Ron. The party awaits us. Oh, stop at the gas station up there and let me grab some ice. I know the guy who works there, and he can tell us if we're going the right way."

"I know where we're going!" Ron shot back.

Clint's wife had remained silent but decided to speak up to ease the tension. "We'll get there soon enough. Let's all just get along and enjoy our time together."

Ron started to slow down again while looking at the street signs. Amy began to lightly bang her head against the passenger-door window as she mumbled, "Why does he always have to drive?"

Each social style responds to different situations in different ways. Ron is a classic Analytical, Amy is a classic Driver, Clint is a classic Expressive, and Clint's wife is a classic Amiable.

Whether it is driving, shopping, or socializing, the four different styles approach life in different ways. Their perspectives and priorities are different, and this always makes for interesting interaction! This chapter examines the four social styles in different settings to show you how they function in real-life situations.

Driving Down the Road

Each social style has distinct driving tendencies. Analyticals are not afraid to use maps and love to navigate. They know exactly how much gas mileage the vehicle gets, and they will drive around forever trying to get the best price on gas. They plan trips with great fervor and annoy other people with too much detail. Analyticals get annoyed by drivers who cut people off and are in a big hurry.

Drivers are the ones who refuse to come to a complete stop at a stop sign. They are usually found speeding past other cars. They are always in a hurry to get to their next task. Drivers like to be in control when driving and get annoyed by people who try to tell them where to go or what to do. Drivers will speed up before they will let someone in their lane. They get annoyed by other drivers who do let people cut in. Drivers are also the ones to wait until the last minute to move over when two lanes merge into one lane. Drivers do not make very good passengers because they like to be in control.

Amiables are the ones who are always letting people cut in front of them. They drive slowly and are annoyed by pushy drivers. Amiables are also the ones who are always waving you to go first at a four-way stop sign. They get nervous about crazy drivers and become fearful and anxious passengers. Amiables feel frustrated with a Driver or Expressive passenger who is pushing them to go faster or telling them how to drive.

Expressives are usually the ones driving down the road with their blinker on. They are too busy talking or singing with the radio to notice! You will also find them with seat belts hanging out the door, lighting sparks on the pavement, because they are distracted by something else. Expressives are the ones who wave their arms and scream and yell when you cut them off or take the right-of-way. Expressives often miss their exit or forget where they are going because they are talking too much or get distracted. They are the consummate backseat drivers!

Going Out to Dinner

Grab the four social styles and go to a restaurant. This is what you can expect: The Analyticals will scrutinize the menu even though they have been there ten times before. They will take forever to order, and they are usually the ones who ask the waitress for "a few more minutes, please." Everything looks so good, and they cannot make up their mind.

Drivers, on the other hand, usually know what they are going to order before they ever get to the restaurant. If they have never been there, they will peruse the menu at top speed, toss it to the side, and proclaim they are ready to order. They consume their food at top speed and are ready to leave before anyone else. Drivers view eating as another task, and when it is over, there are better things to do than just sit at a table.

Amiables will eat just about anywhere and anything—not necessarily because they like it, but because they do not want to hurt anyone's feelings or cause conflict. They are usually the ones at the table who ask everyone, "What are you having?" Even if the service is terrible, Amiables feel bad if no one wants to leave a tip. Amiables do not like to send food back, even if it is not what they ordered. They are the best listeners for the Expressives in the group. Amiables love to study the people at their table and the people around them.

Expressives have a great time wherever they go. They do not care if they have been there before or if it is a new place. They love to try new things and appreciate a wide variety of foods. They are usually the ones to order the really weird items on the menu. They figure, "What the heck—you only live once!" Expressives take a long time to order because they may be too busy talking to everyone at the table (or even to strangers at the next table) to look at the menu. They will eat fast if there is a party to go to where there will be lots of people. Other times it will take them forever to finish their meal because there is so much conversation at the table.

Social Gatherings

At a social gathering like a party, Analyticals will usually spend most of their time with one or two people in quality conversation. They like to analyze the topics of discussion and interject some of their critical thinking.

Drivers will move into a group and slowly overpower it. They are not as opinionated in large groups as they are individually, but they will still offer their opinions. Some of their sarcasm will usually emerge in group settings as they become more comfortable.

If Amiables decide to join a group in a social setting, they usually participate by active listening. Sometimes they will not even join a group. Instead, they will sit on the sidelines and watch. They love to observe human behavior. They are usually apprehended by Expressives who discover a willing ear.

Expressives will often enter the party mouth-first. They usually talk to every person there before they leave. They are great storytellers and tend to hold everyone's attention. Expressives are usually "the life of the party," and can be very entertaining.

Putting a Swing Set Together

If you asked each of the four social styles to assemble a swing set, you would come up with varied results. The Analyticals would open the box and read the instructions first. Then they may read them again to be sure they understand everything. Next, they would put all the parts in order and begin to assemble the swing set exactly as instructed. Analyticals would take forever to finish the job, but the end result would be a perfectly assembled swing set.

The Driver would rip open the box, pull out the instructions, and toss them off to the side! Drivers hate manuals and rarely ever read them, except maybe as a last resort. Drivers will dump all the parts on the ground in a pile. They would assemble the swing set by intuition and at top speed. When they are done, they usually have a few nuts and bolts left over, but their theory is "the swing set works, so who cares!"

Amiables read the instructions and then hire an Analytical to put it together. They usually solicit input from family members as to where it should be placed. They are concerned with what other people think. If they do not like the way the swing set was put together, they usually will not say anything.

Expressives will not read the instructions either. They will stand over the box of parts for a while complaining about having to put it together. Then they will go find a few neighbors to do it for them. They may hand the assemblers an occasional screwdriver while talking their ears off. Expressives will then invite half of the neighborhood over for a "swing-set party" and brag about the swing set they put together.

Social Styles in Church

Every person takes his or her own social style everywhere—this includes church. Every church on the face of the earth has conflict to address as a direct result of social-style conflicts. Hurt feelings occur for a variety of reasons:

+ Some people think deductively and some think intuitively.

+ Some people are letter-of-the-law (task-oriented) believers, and some are spirit-of-the-law (relationship-oriented) believers.

+ Some people are slow-paced—embracing tradition and sameness, and some are fast-paced—preferring new methods and ideas.

+ Some people are more reserved in their worship style (askers) while others are more outgoing (tellers).

Think about your own church for a moment. Is your pastor a Driver, Analytical, Amiable, or Expressive? Do you think entire churches can take on a basic social style based on the pastor or the church board? Are some churches more Expressive in nature, while others are more Analytical? Can you begin to see where some pace-and-priority conflict problems exist within your own church?

What about when a pastor leaves? If you had an easygoing and caring Amiable pastor and then switched to a fast-paced, task-oriented Driver who thrived on change, do you think the church would experience conflict? Absolutely.

People butt heads in church and struggle with conflict just as much as they do in the corporate setting. Hopefully, practicing the fruit of the Spirit gives an advantage to Christians! "But the fruit of the Spirit is love, joy, peace, patience, kindness, goodness, faithfulness, gentleness and self-control" (Galatians 5:22-23).

All four social styles need to display all of the qualities listed in Galatians. However, by nature, certain social styles will struggle more with the expression of some qualities:

+ Analyticals need to work on expressing joy and faith.

+ Drivers need to work on expressing patience and gentleness.

+ Amiables need to work on expressing endurance and peace.

+ Expressives need to work on expressing faithfulness and self-control.

Your positive, loving social style behavior can be a benefit to your church. Or your negative, selfish social-style behavior can be the source of disharmony, disunity, and disaster wherever you go. As you allow the Spirit of God to work in you, focus on manifesting the positive traits of your social style and minimizing the negative.

8

Identifying Social Styles in Others

Even a child is known by his actions.
—Proverbs 20:11

—*m*—

After presenting the social-styles concept to a church gathering, one of the attendees approached me and said,

I can really see how some of the people in my life fit into each social-style category. I'm an Analytical, and now I can see that my wife is a Driver. I make decisions too slowly for her, and she is too abrupt at times for me. We both like getting things accomplished though, so we have a lot in common there. My boss is an Expressive and fits the descriptions perfectly! She makes decisions based on emotion and gut feelings, and that doesn't always sit well with me. I love her excitement and charisma, though. My mom is an Amiable, and my Dad is an Analytical. I can see now why they've had conflict in some areas. It's amazing how it all makes sense now.

That is one of the reasons this approach to social styles is so widely accepted and embraced. It is simple to recognize social styles in other people. You do not need your family, friends, and co-workers to fill out a ten-page questionnaire to figure out what social style they have. You can determine their social style by observing their behavior.

At one conference I spoke at, I gave a 45-minute presentation on the social styles. It was fast, fun, and full of humor. I asked everyone to break into respective social-style groups, and it was interesting to observe the behavior of each group. As they began to organize themselves, the Amiables were being kind and accommodating. The Drivers were giving clear direction on what to do and taking the bull by the horns. The Analyticals were discussing how they saw themselves as a little of each style. The Expressives took their chairs and started to form a circle where they could see each other and talk. They were having fun and laughing loudly.

When I pointed out that we were all going to keep our chairs facing forward, the Expressives began to laugh even more. I pointed out that only the Expressive group would think to gather their chairs like that so they could be extra social! As you become more and more familiar with the behaviors of each social style, it becomes easier to identify who they are. It gave each group an opportunity to immediately see how differently each social style behaves in certain circumstances.

Once I was teaching a class at a conference, and I decided to visit some of the other classes during my downtime. I went from classroom to classroom, listening to the different instructors. I observed the styles of the instructors and how they all interacted with the audience. After sitting in each class for about 15 minutes, I was able to identify the different social styles.

One instructor used a large number of graphs and statistics. The presentation was extremely thorough and factual. The instructor was very credible and made sure every detail was provided on the subject. He moved slowly and methodically through the material. He answered questions from the audience in a very detailed and articulate manner. He was an Analytical.

One of the other instructors had the room in stitches. He was hysterical! He was loud, gregarious, and told lots of funny stories about the people with whom he worked. Classes down the hall could hear his presentation. He spoke at top speed and rarely took a breath. He gave his opinion quite often and loved to engage the audience. He allowed the break to go extra long and seemed to be pretty relaxed about how the class was structured. He was an Expressive.

Another instructor started the session exactly on time. She was very articulate and carried herself with a tremendous amount of confidence. She projected a sense of leadership and authority. She made her points quickly and concisely. She did not belabor any of her points and stayed on track with her presentation. She handled audience questions with confidence and self-assurance. She spoke her mind and did not seem to be concerned with what everyone thought about it. She was a Driver.

I observed yet another instructor who was the friendliest person at the conference. He was thanking everyone as they came in the door. Throughout the presentation, he was checking with the audience to make sure the temperature was comfortable. He appeared tentative at times when answering questions. When someone challenged his position, he seemed to get very uncomfortable and unsure of himself. He was soft-spoken and moved slowly through his presentation. He projected a sense of warmth and caring to the audience. He was an Amiable.

As you learn to correlate specific behaviors with the specific social styles, you will see how easy it is to identify the social styles of people. The charts below list some famous individuals and their corresponding social styles. As you review the four different categories, think about some of the traits they share.

Famous Analyticals	
✦ Albert Einstein	✦ Woodrow Wilson
✦ Sherlock Holmes	✦ Spock ("Star Trek")
✦ Confucius	✦ Isaac Newton
✦ William Shakespeare	✦ Moses
✦ Agatha Christie	✦ Charles Darwin
✦ William Buckley (writer)	✦ The apostle Thomas
✦ Billy Crystal	✦ The Gospel-writer Luke

Chart 8-A

Famous Drivers	
✦ Napoleon	✦ Bill O'Reilly
✦ The apostle Paul	✦ Dr. McCoy ("Star Trek")
✦ Adolph Hitler	✦ Margaret Thatcher
✦ Richard Nixon	✦ Henry Ford
✦ Clint Eastwood	✦ Martin Luther King
✦ Lucy (Peanuts comic strip)	✦ Harrison Ford
✦ Jacob (Bible)	✦ Rush Limbaugh

Chart 8-B

Famous Amiables	
✦ Jimmy Carter	✦ Winnie the Pooh
✦ Abraham (Bible)	✦ Mother Teresa
✦ Gerald Ford	✦ Dick Clark
✦ Bill Cosby	✦ John Denver
✦ Scotty ("Star Trek")	✦ Princess Diana
✦ Gandhi	✦ Esther (Bible)
✦ John Candy	✦ Dale Carnegie

Chart 8-C

Famous Expressives	
✦ Bob Hope	✦ Don Knotts
✦ Robin Williams	✦ Jim Carrey
✦ Bill Clinton	✦ Ronald Reagan
✦ Captain Kirk ("Star Trek")	✦ Carol Burnett
✦ Lucille Ball	✦ Joan Rivers
✦ Donald Duck	✦ Jack Berry
✦ Jezebel (Bible)	✦ The apostle Peter

Chart 8-D

Each social style manifests certain behaviors that can easily be identified. Below is a chart of common behaviors that each social style possesses. As you review the lists, write down some people you work with or live with and see if you can identify their social style.

Analyticals		
✦ Think before they speak ✦ Talk softly and slowly ✦ Eat slowly ✦ Perform tasks with deliberation ✦ Follow instructions ✦ Thrive on facts ✦ Enjoy details ✦ Display good manners ✦ Dress conservatively ✦ Are on time or early	✦ Do not display emotion ✦ Make thoughtful decisions ✦ Are private ✦ Can be overly critical ✦ Stay extremely focused ✦ Want things done correctly the first time ✦ Stay organized ✦ Examine all possible alternatives	✦ Play the devil's advocate ✦ Are "letter of the law" people ✦ Can be tenacious ✦ Are very responsible ✦ Remain loyal ✦ Seem serious or aloof ✦ Are perfectionists ✦ Like planning ✦ Can be nagging ✦ Can be narrow-minded

Chart 8-E

Analyticals in my life:_____

_____

_____

_____

Drivers

- Speak before they think
- Talk quickly and boldly
- Eat quickly
- Can perform many tasks at once
- Can be insensitive
- Make direct eye contact
- Dislike details
- Tend to intimidate people
- Are on time or early
- Do not display emotion

- Make quick decisions
- Like to lead
- Can overpower people
- Are fearless
- Do not like chitchat
- Possess high energy
- Dress powerfully
- Are opinionated
- Can be obstinate
- Face conflict head-on
- Are impatient

- Despise excuses
- Can be intolerant
- Appear arrogant
- Can be belligerent
- Are very confident
- Show great initiative
- Have tremendous willpower
- Work at top speed
- Are very sarcastic

Chart 8-F

Drivers in my life: _____

_____

_____

_____

Amiables		
◆ Speak with a friendly tone ◆ Talk softly and slowly ◆ Are great listeners ◆ Like to please people ◆ Prefer to follow ◆ Like to volunteer ◆ Dislike conflict ◆ Are very courteous ◆ Avoid decisions ◆ Seek approval ◆ Are very humble	◆ Possess extreme patience ◆ Avoid attention ◆ Encourage people ◆ Are generous and giving ◆ Can make excuses ◆ Are very cooperative ◆ Do not like criticism ◆ Are very likeable ◆ Can be insecure ◆ Can be overly dependent	◆ Move in a slow manner ◆ Can be overly sensitive ◆ Are not assertive ◆ Display loyalty ◆ Are diplomatic ◆ Value cooperation ◆ Put people before tasks ◆ Show compassion ◆ Can be procrastinators

Chart 8-G

Amiables in my life: _____

_____

_____

_____

Expressives

✦ Speak before they think ✦ Talk quickly and loudly ✦ Eat quickly ✦ Are visionaries ✦ Adapt to anything ✦ Are overly relaxed about time ✦ Can be undisciplined ✦ Are big risk-takers ✦ Have a hard time following through	✦ Dress unusually ✦ Have short attention spans ✦ Are unpredictable ✦ Love spontaneity ✦ Are very enthusiastic ✦ Have high energy ✦ Love to talk ✦ Dismiss what other people think ✦ Tell it like it is ✦ Dislike details ✦ Like to socialize	✦ Are creative and imaginative ✦ Are outspoken and outgoing ✦ Can be rebellious ✦ Motivate and inspire people ✦ Possess flexibility ✦ Prone to exaggeration ✦ Lack focus ✦ Have a great sense of humor ✦ Dislike rules

Chart 8-H

Expressives in my life: _____

_____

_____

_____

Although every social style will possess a secondary style, the predominant style is not hard to identify once you become familiar with the basic characteristics of each style. As you can see by the previous social-style boxes, each style displays very distinct behaviors.

The Analyticals and Amiables are slower and quieter in their speech and movements. They are both askers and are not very outgoing or outspoken. Drivers and Expressives move faster and speak louder. They are both tellers and are more assertive, outspoken, and outgoing.

The Analyticals and Drivers are both task-oriented and less relationship-oriented. They both appreciate getting things done, although at different paces. Analyticals and Drivers are not emotional creatures and make decisions with their heads and not their guts.

Amiables and Expressives are both relationship-oriented and less task-oriented. They place people ahead of projects. Amiables and Expressives are more emotional in nature and make decisions based on a gut feeling.

Why is it important to learn how to identify the social styles in people? Because you can predict future behavior and respond accordingly once you have identified a person's social style. The ability to adapt to the behavior of other people will only serve to reduce the potential conflict that inevitably arises.

9

What Annoying People Value and What *Really* Annoys Them

He that wrestles with us, strengthens
our nerves, and sharpens our skill.
Our antagonist is our helper.
—EDMUND BURKE

———

We were midway through the leadership training in a corporation. I asked all the participants to write down what they valued most. Then I asked them to make a list of some of the things that annoyed them the most.

After the exercise was completed, we had a time of discussion where we shared some of our answers. While some things were valued by everyone (like honesty, love, etc.), other things were a higher priority to some people than to others. What annoyed everyone was different as well.

The Analyticals valued accuracy, competence, and organization. They appreciated facts, efficiency, quality, and structure. On the top of their annoyance list were things like disorganization, hastiness, and aggressiveness. They were especially annoyed by shouting, invasiveness, and exaggeration.

The Drivers seemed to value achievement, goals, responsibility, and independence. Productivity was important to them, as was speed and control. Drivers were easily annoyed by indecisiveness, procrastination, and laziness. They also did not appreciate excuses, hypersensitivity, or too many details.

The Amiables valued contribution, compassion, and loyalty. Trust, kindness, and peacefulness made the top of their priority lists. They also valued cooperation and friendliness. As nice as Amiables can be, they still have a list of things that annoy them. Conflict, pressure, and harshness all made the top of the list. They were also annoyed by rudeness, pushiness, and disharmony.

Expressives seemed to value excitement, adventure, and spontaneity. They also placed innovation, vision, and creativity at the top of their lists. They had plenty of items that caused them to become annoyed. Formality, rules, and structure seemed to be big annoyances. Routine, boredom, details, and ritual all made the list as well.

As we all compared notes, everyone began to see the links between the social styles and the common threads of what they valued. The attendees were able to make a connection between each social style and what seemed to be the biggest annoyances. The lightbulbs started to go on. People were beginning to realize where some of the conflict and misunderstandings were coming from. They did not all value the same things, and they did not all appreciate the same behaviors. While one social style may welcome someone who really "tells it like it is," that can be a point of contention for another social style.

Each social style values different things, and different things annoy each social style. There is a well-known saying, "Treat others as you would want to be treated." In theory, this is a great idea; however, when it comes to the four social styles, it would be much better to treat other people how *they* want to be treated, not how *you* want to be treated. Until you discover what each style values and despises, it is very difficult to create a cohesive working or personal relationship with each social style. Review the charts below for an overview of what each style values and finds annoying.

Analyticals	
What They Value	**What Annoys Them**
✦ Security	✦ Inaccuracy
✦ Accuracy	✦ Incompetence
✦ Stability	✦ Change
✦ Rules and regulations	✦ Aggressiveness
✦ Quality	✦ Shouting
✦ Structure	✦ Evasiveness
✦ Efficiency	✦ Mediocrity
✦ Facts	✦ Inadequacy
✦ Competence	✦ Exaggeration
✦ Details	✦ Invasiveness
✦ Tradition	✦ Clutter
✦ Critical thinking	✦ Disorganization
✦ Organization	✦ Clamor
✦ Logic	✦ Hastiness

Chart 9-A

Drivers	
What They Value	**What Annoys Them**
✦ Achievement	✦ Indecisiveness
✦ Challenge	✦ Boredom
✦ Success	✦ Small talk
✦ Power	✦ Details
✦ Speed	✦ Hypersensitivity
✦ Control	✦ Overemotionalism
✦ Responsibility	✦ Dependency
✦ Goals	✦ Excuses
✦ Debates	✦ Irresponsibility
✦ Competition	✦ Lethargy
✦ Leadership	✦ Laziness
✦ Independence	✦ Procrastination
✦ Decisiveness	✦ Taking orders
✦ Productivity	✦ Overanalysis

Chart 9-B

Amiables	
What They Value	**What Annoys Them**
✦ Contribution	✦ Conflict
✦ Comfort	✦ Impatience
✦ Compassion	✦ Disrespect
✦ Cooperation	✦ Discourteousness
✦ Friendliness	✦ Insensitivity
✦ Peacefulness	✦ Harshness
✦ Loyalty	✦ Rushing
✦ Approval	✦ Pressure
✦ Cohesiveness	✦ Tension
✦ Trust	✦ Controversy
✦ Kindness	✦ Disharmony
✦ Relationships	✦ Yelling
✦ Benevolence	✦ Pushiness
✦ Coaching	✦ Rudeness

Chart 9-C

Expressives	
What They Value	**What Annoys Them**
✦ Freedom	✦ Rules
✦ Excitement	✦ Structure
✦ Adventure	✦ Schedules
✦ Flexibility	✦ Routine
✦ Spontaneity	✦ Tedium
✦ Vision	✦ Stagnation
✦ Enthusiasm	✦ Slowness
✦ Change	✦ Boredom
✦ Unpredictability	✦ Ritual
✦ Uniqueness	✦ Lack of originality
✦ Creativity	✦ Lack of creativity
✦ Innovation	✦ Details
✦ Versatility	✦ Formality

Chart 9-E

As you examine the values and annoyances of each style, you can begin to see where each style has the potential to rub the other styles the wrong way. This is also why everyone has the potential to be annoying! The very thing you value may be an annoyance to another style.

The Driver values decisiveness, and the Analytical is annoyed when pushed to make a decision. The Expressive values a fast pace, and the Amiable gets annoyed with impatience and likes to take things in stride. Every social style exhibits some form of behavior that has the potential to annoy all three other styles.

If you know what annoys the other styles, you can modify your behavior to stop annoying them. If you know what the other styles value, you can modify your behavior to get along better and make them happy. Part II will address more specifically how to adapt to meet the specific needs of each style to prevent and resolve conflict.

10

Annoying People with Their Backs Against the Wall

An offended brother is more unyielding
than a fortified city, and disputes are like the
barred gates of a citadel.
—PROVERBS 18:19

———

Erin tried to listen patiently, but Bob was beginning to become irrational. He was attacking her and chewing her out with gusto. She tried to get up and leave the room, but he only followed her. "Don't try to run away from this problem like you always do!" Bob continued to yell, as she walked out of the room. This seemed to be the constant cycle they both fell into when conflict would arise.

Erin would normally retreat, and Bob would blow up. Bob wanted to confront the issues head-on, and Erin wanted time to think things through and not be pushed to make a decision. Erin felt that Bob came on way too strong, and Bob felt that Erin should take a stand. Neither one of them appreciated the way the other one responded to conflict.

Each social style has a specific response to conflict. The Analyticals will withdraw in an attempt to save face and think through the problem. They avoid and dodge the undesirable situation and are annoyed by people who come on too strong.

The Drivers will attempt to control the person or situation. They tend to impose their thoughts and opinions on other people in the midst of conflict. If they feel they are losing control, they tend to overcontrol to compensate. They are very strong-willed individuals and can become demanding during conflict.

The Amiables will give in to avoid the confrontation. They do not feel the conflict is worth it. They would rather save the relationship, even if it hurts them. Amiables appear to be in agreement on the outside, but may be resentful on the inside.

Expressives will attack in the midst of conflict. They may use condemnations and put-downs to discredit people. They have very strong emotions and feelings and will let others know exactly what they think. Expressives can chew people out and have a tendency to raise their voices when conflict escalates.

Chart 10-A shows the different responses to conflict of each social style.

Analyticals: Withdraw	Drivers: Dominate
They tend to become less assertive, more controlled, hold in feelings, and not share ideas. Basically, they avoid, dodge, escape, and retreat from other people and/or undesirable situations.	They tend to become overassertive, unbending, overcontrolling and demanding. They are strong-willed and attempt to impose their thoughts and feelings on people.
Amiables: Give In	Expressives: Attack
They tend to give in to keep the peace and reduce conflict. They appear to agree with other people when on the inside they disagree. They strongly desire to save the relationship even if it hurts them.	They tend to emotionally attack people and their ideas, using condemnations and put-downs to discredit them. They have strong emotions and will tell people how they feel about things.

Chart 10-A

Back-Against-the-Wall Behavior

Each social style has a set of positive and negative behaviors. When the pressures of interpersonal conflict arise, we tend to feel like our backs are against the wall. Once this happens, we tend to shift from the positive side of our traits to the negative. We become more extreme and rigid and less flexible as we move into nonnegotiable stances. As a result, our interaction with people becomes counterproductive.

Analyticals, who are characteristically precise and systematic, become inflexible and nitpicky, choosing to withdraw or evade the problems. Determined and objective Drivers turn into domineering, unfeeling dictators. Amiables, who are usually supportive and easygoing, become permissive and conforming as they just give in during conflict. Expressives, who are generally enthusiastic and imaginative, become overbearing and unrealistic, resorting to explosive attacks on people.

As we focus on our own needs and seek relief from tension by manifesting our negative behaviors, tension rises in those around us. As a result, other people become defensive and switch to their own back-against-the-wall behaviors. This domino effect of setting each other off leads to more disagreements, arguments, fights, and even wars.

As we discussed earlier, every social style will have an initial back-against-the-wall response to conflict. If that response does not relieve the tension or solve the conflict, each social style will resort to a second choice. If that does not work, a third choice will be employed, and then a fourth. Each social style has an ordered pattern for moving through a series of back-against-the-wall responses. For example, when a Driver experiences conflict, his first response would be to try and dominate the situation or persons involved. If that does not work, he will likely withdraw from the situation. If that does not solve the conflict, he may attack those he blames for the problem. The last resort for a Driver is to give in. If he cannot win the confrontation, the Driver will finally give up and give in. Chart 10-B lists the common order of negative responses for each social style.

Analyticals	Drivers
1. Withdraw	1. Dominate
2. Dominate	2. Withdraw
3. Give In	3. Attack
4. Attack	4. Give In
Amiables	**Expressives**
1. Give In	1. Attack
2. Attack	2. Give In
3. Withdraw	3. Dominate
4. Dominate	4. Withdraw

Robert Bolton and Dorothy G. Bolton, *Social Style/Management Style* (New York: AMACOM, 1984), adapted from p. 48.

Chart 10-B

Responding to Each Social Style in Conflict

As you can see, each social style responds differently to conflict when pushed. You will have your own response as well, which may only serve to escalate the conflict. Learning to respond to each social style in conflict will reduce tension and go a long way toward resolving the conflict.

Responding to the Withdrawing Analytical

As we observed earlier, Analyticals tend to withdraw from conflict to save face. They want to deal with the problem alone, with a minimum amount of interaction with people. They need time to think about the problem, situation, or relationship. They need as much information as possible in order to deal effectively with their distress.

Do not keep pushing Analyticals for a response or insist on their increased participation before they have adequate time to think. They need time and space, so give it to them. Since Analyticals are systematic by nature, make sure you approach their problem with a step-by-step solution. Help them set up a plan to gather more problem-solving data to consider. Ask them for a special time to discuss the matter after they have had time to think things through.

If you are an Expressive or a Driver, your natural tendency is to tell, not ask. If you want to reduce conflict with the Analytical, practice patience. Learn to speak softer, slower, and ask questions. "What ideas do you have for a solution? How do you feel about doing A, B, and C?" When you approach Analyticals with a step-by-step solution for review, you are talking their language.

Responding to the Dominating Driver

Drivers feel like they have lost control in conflict situations, leaving them with no personal choices. The tension they feel drives them to get something accomplished, and they may attempt to regain control by overcontrolling.

Do not try to compete with Drivers or match force with force, because competition is their specialty. Do not argue or debate with them. They can verbally shred you to pieces in a matter of seconds. But do not back down from them either, even when they come on strong. Drivers respect people who hold their ground, even if that person disagrees with their position. They just do not want you attempting to persuade them to abandon their own position.

When in the midst of conflict with Drivers, do not inundate them with too much detail or take too long to get to the point. They will get very irritated and even cut you off to get something accomplished. Try to redirect the strong energies of the Driver toward positive goals, achievements, or actions that you can support. Drivers appreciate goals and the freedom to choose their own methods of reaching them. Help them decide on a goal and a path for it. Attempting to control Drivers will only cause more conflict and cause them to overcontrol.

Responding to the Acquiescing Amiable

During conflict, Amiables will always appear to be in agreement. They will try to maintain relationships at all costs, even at the cost of personal hurt. A gentleman approached me after a seminar and said,

> I realize now that my former wife was an Amiable. We never really fought, because as soon as we would get into conflict, she would always agree with me. It always seemed like everything was fine. She saw things my way, and we got along great. At least, that is what I thought. After 11 years, I came home one day and all her stuff was packed and she was gone. She left a note saying she couldn't take it anymore. All along I thought we were doing just fine, but she was miserable and didn't want to rock the boat. I wish I knew then what I know now.

A sign of compliance and agreement by the Amiable is not a sign of commitment. They often have inner turmoil that they do not want to share. They fear backlash or continued conflict if they share what they really think. Consequently, they simply agree with the person with whom they are in conflict and give in.

If you are in conflict with Amiables, do not push them for a response. Amiables do not appreciate people who come on too strong. Do not express anger or raise your voice. Do not argue with them or insist on your way. This will only push them deeper into their pattern of acquiescence as they struggle to save the relationship. Instead, encourage them to share their feelings. Ask them for constructive criticism regarding the conflict. If they get the courage to actually tell you, do not make them sorry they did! Do not belittle them or negate their input, or you may never get it again.

Amiables like to feel that they are needed and can help people out. Tell them that you would like to work on the conflict situation, but you need some concrete suggestions from them. Work side by side with them through the problem-solving steps they suggest. Establish some form of evaluation process. They will respond cautiously, so move slowly and be patient.

Responding to the Attacking Expressive

Expressives become very selfish, emotional, and assertive when their backs are against the wall. They will vent their feelings by attacking the situation and the people involved. They will not hesitate in telling you what they really think, and they will do it with gusto!

Do not try to evaluate the emotional outburst of an Expressive. It will not help to defend yourself intellectually either. Do not let Expressives draw you into their tantrums. Do not try to outshout an Expressive because you will most likely lose. Instead, try to listen sympathetically and accept their emotions without getting emotionally involved.

Let them get their emotions out of their system. If you block the venting of the Expressives, you may provoke an even greater explosion. Once they get their emotions off their chest, you can help them focus on creative alternatives for handling problems in the future. You might try something like, "Now that you have shared your feelings about it, how are we going to handle this problem the next time it comes up?" Expressives are creative individuals. Once they move out of the negative behaviors they exhibit when their backs are against the wall, they will return to their positive dispositions.

Adapting to Meet the Needs of Each Social Style to Reduce Conflict

The best way to avoid having to deal with back-against-the-wall behavior is to prevent it as much as possible. The best way to prevent most negative conflict is to adapt to meet the needs of people. If you want to get along better with the people with whom you live and work, you will employ this technique. Each social style thinks and operates differently. If you want to create a cohesive relationship, you can adapt to each style.

Adapting to Meet the Needs of the Analyticals

1. Analyticals are askers and do not appreciate people who come on too strong or are pushy. Speak softly and slowly to Analyticals.

2. Analyticals are more task-oriented and appreciate discussions about achievements. Talk to them about reachable goals.

3. Analyticals are deductive thinkers. Be sure to meet their needs for facts, time lines, and step-by-step procedures.

4. Do not expect quick decisions from Analyticals. Give them time to reflect and evaluate information before they decide.

5. Analyticals have a strong need to be correct and make the right decisions. They would rather make no decision than a wrong one. Help them realize that it is impossible to make perfect decisions all the time. Help them relax and encourage them in the decision-making process.

6. Analyticals want to know how things work. They appreciate getting detailed instructions, and they like to give them.

7. Analyticals sometimes feel awkward in relationships. Help them save face by not putting too much pressure on them in social settings.

8. Exercise patience when dealing with Analyticals. When they talk, they often give out more information than necessary. They will explain their position with great detail. Their presentations of material may be so loaded with facts and detail that the ideas become difficult to follow. You may need to listen to more material than you would like in order to assure Analyticals that you are listening and you care.

9. Do not try to oversell your ideas or overstate your positions to Analyticals. They have a strong sense of logic and can quickly identify reasonable facts. Be sure you provide facts when making your case. Be clear and specific.

10. Encourage and praise Analyticals for their wise planning, efficient techniques, and conservative nature.

Adapting to Meet the Needs of the Drivers

1. Drivers are tellers and appreciate people who make their points clearly and concisely. Try not to bore them with a lot of detail. Get to your bottom line quickly.

2. Drivers are intuitive thinkers and will trust their hunches. Do not give them a big sales pitch. If your ideas or suggestions seem valid, Drivers will immediately accept them. However, they may not admit the validity of your ideas or give you credit because they like to remain in control.

3. Since Drivers like to feel in control, let them choose their methods or paths of response. Tell them the goal you would like to achieve and give them options or alternatives for reaching that goal. Let them use the information to chart their own course, and do not try to control them.

4. Drivers want to know what is going on, what needs to be accomplished, and what your ideas are. They are interested in the answers to how, who, why, and when questions. Be sure to let them know what your expectations are. They will tell you if they can or will reach those expectations.

5. Drivers struggle with impatience. Since they process information and accomplish tasks quickly, they do not have much patience with those who think or work slowly. Try to increase your pace around Drivers. They appreciate saving time because they want to get on to their many tasks.

6. Since Drivers move at such a quick pace, try to keep your relationships with them businesslike. If Drivers seem a little cold and matter-of-fact, try not to take it personally. They tend to be much more concerned with accomplishments and achievements than relationships. They look for results.

7. Encourage and praise Drivers for all the jobs and tasks they get done. But do not overdo the encouragement. They will be off and running to accomplish something else before you finish your statement of appreciation.

Adapting to Meet the Needs of the Amiables

1. Amiables are askers and they appreciate people who are gentle and not brash.

2. Amiables do not offer hasty opinions or make quick decisions. They do not want to do or say something that might hamper their relationships. Help them realize that sharing their thoughts will not affect their relationship with you.

3. Amiables ask, "Why?" They need information that will explain why they should do something. Explain to them what effort they need to put forth on a particular task or project. Help them see how they will benefit from it and how their participation will help other people.

4. Amiables have a hard time really relaxing in social situations. They do not want to say or do anything that might cause tension. Encourage them to see that a disagreement with someone is not the end of the world. Help them realize that it is possible for people to hold different opinions and yet still remain friends.

5. Amiables do not like to work alone. They need a good deal of encouragement and assurance. Amiables need to feel like they are part of a team and that their input matters. Let them work with you.

6. Amiables like to know that they are accepted. Take the time to show personal interest in their lives.

7. Amiables are hesitant to share their opinion. Learn to be patient in communicating with them. Try not to disagree with them in public or when you suspect a disagreement will hurt their feelings. Otherwise, they will clam up and not share anything with you.

8. If you hope to get Amiables to participate, clearly define what you expect from them. Communicate to them what you plan to do to contribute to the relationship or the task at hand.

9. Encourage and praise Amiables with warm personal thanks for their contributions and participation.

Adapting to Meet the Needs of the Expressives

1. Expressives are tellers and they appreciate people who will listen to them and share with them. Become involved with their interests as much as possible.

2. Expressives are intuitive thinkers. They process information and form judgments and opinions quickly. They will also share their opinions openly. Have patience with their quick decisions. They operate at a feeling level and may not always be able to give you a rational explanation for their behavior.

3. Expressives have a tendency to "tell it like it is." Try not to take their comments personally. Many times, they are simply letting off steam, and you may just happen to be in the path.

4. Expressives are relationship-oriented, and they want to know who is going to be involved. Try to meet their needs for excitement and interaction with people.

5. Expressives tend to start many jobs and not complete them. Try to work with them to accomplish tasks and see things through. They like to visit with other people while they are working and do not perform at their best level if working alone.

6. Expressives tend to exaggerate and overgeneralize. Be alert to, and patient with, their overstatements.

7. Expressives become easily sidetracked. Try to help them complete the task they start. They like to anticipate the future. Share in their excitement for what lies ahead.

8. Encourage and praise Expressives for their enthusiasm. Publicly recognize them and show appreciation for jobs well done.

The reason we wrestle with selfishness, weakness, and conflict in our relationships is because we all inherited something more than our social styles. Thanks to Adam, we have also inherited a sin nature. Consequently, it is the nature of man to be sinful and selfish, just as surely as it is the nature of a pig to wallow in the mud. People do not need to learn to sin anymore than pigs need to learn to wallow; we do it naturally.

The social styles of behavior have both positive and negative traits. Our sin nature pulls us to exercise the negative traits of our social style. Even when we are exercising positive traits, the sin nature is still encouraging us to use those traits for selfish reasons. In one ear we hear Jesus telling us to "love your neighbor as yourself," but in the other ear the sin nature chimes in with, "Look out for number one!" It is very clear that the old nature is not going to help us with Christ's command. We need a new nature that is equipped with the ability to get along with people. We need a new nature that strengthens our strengths and weakens our weaknesses. We need a nature motivated by God Himself.

This new nature comes only when you begin to love God with all your heart, soul, and mind. How can you love God this way? How can you find peace with God and your fellow man? It starts by confessing to God that you are a sinner in need of a Savior. When you invite Jesus Christ into your heart and life, you will have the Spirit of God dwelling in you. He is that very Spirit that begins to do a work in your heart and life, and facilitates the change in your old behavior as you become a new creation in Christ.

When we receive Christ into our lives, we receive a new nature. This new nature empowers the positive traits and behaviors of our social style while battling the negative. Our motivation is no longer controlled by the old nature, resulting in ungodly behavior, but is now motivated by genuine love, resulting in godly behavior. The old nature does not just die instantly or give up that easily. Our lives become a constant battleground between the old nature and the new nature, negative behaviors and positive behaviors, strengths and weaknesses.

Through the power of the Holy Spirit, we can fight the daily battle and learn to manifest our strengths and minimize our weaknesses. As we do, we will discover a positive change in our relationships and a stark improvement in the quality of our lives.

11

How to Lead Annoying People

Learning is the essential fuel for the leader, the source of high-octane energy that keeps up the momentum by continually sparking new understanding, new ideas, and new challenges. It is absolutely indispensable under today's conditions of rapid change and complexity. Very simply, those who do not learn do not long survive as leaders.
—Warren Bennis and Burt Nanus

———

How exactly do you get so many people motivated to get involved?" Mike was picking Jamie's brain. They were both on the board of a nonprofit, charitable organization and Jamie seemed to pull off huge events with little effort. She was esteemed as an incredible leader in the community and seemed to be involved in everything, while she was always getting other people involved.

"Don't get me wrong, Mike—it's a lot of work! But I've realized something that makes it much easier. People are motivated by different things. Not everyone thinks and operates like I do. Some people want to be supervised, and others want to be left alone. Some people want a lot of control and responsibility, while others want to serve in a support role. The key is to know the people who follow you so you can lead them according to *their* needs, not yours."

Mike began to realize that his leadership style did not allow much room for individuality. He just expected everyone to do things the way he did. He often became impatient and frustrated when people did not follow, and he was starting to realize why. Leading people required a lot more than just barking out orders and being in a position of power. It required quite the opposite. It required a great deal of understanding and humility. Mike realized it was time to get to know his followers.

Leadership Roles and Styles

During a discussion on the topic of leadership, Henry Ford once said, "Who ought to be the boss is like asking who ought to be the tenor in the quartet—obviously, the man who can sing tenor."

Which social style makes the best leader? It is often assumed that individuals who are more extroverted—the tellers—make better leaders than introverted persons—the askers. This is not a safe assumption. An outspoken person is not necessarily better qualified for leadership.

There is much more to leadership than the ability to state opinions confidently. The exciting thing about the social-styles concept is that effective, successful leaders can be found in all four social styles. Leaders will reflect the characteristics of their particular style: Analytical, Driver, Amiable, or Expressive.

There are many roles that leaders must assume, and some of those roles come more naturally for certain social styles. For the other styles, it is more of a stretch to fulfill some of the leadership responsibilities. Here is a list of the ten main leadership roles that must be assumed by a quality leader:

- ✦ Delegator
- ✦ Facilitator
- ✦ Manager
- ✦ Clarifier
- ✦ Problem-solver

- ✦ Mediator
- ✦ Nurturer
- ✦ Coach
- ✦ Dreamer/Visionary
- ✦ Initiator

As you examine the list, you will see that the role of nurturer comes naturally to the Amiable, but is a stretch for the Driver. Dreamer/Visionary is quite simple for the Expressive, but a challenge for the Analytical. Initiator is a specialty for the Driver, but not so easy for the Amiable. Clarifier is a natural role for an Analytical, but not for an Expressive. Chart 11-A gives a few examples of what comes easier and harder for each social style.

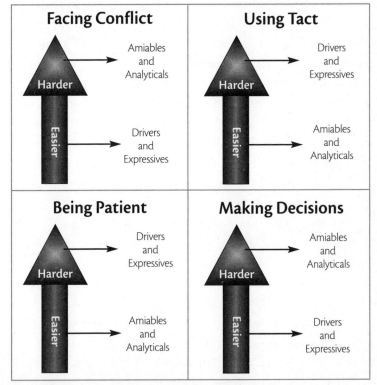

Chart 11-A

True leadership requires characteristics of all social styles and a need for adaptation by the leader. Regardless of your social style, if you are in a leadership position, you need to be aware of the needs and behavioral tendencies of your followers. As we learned in previous sections, each social style values different things and becomes annoyed by different things. Attempting to lead every person with one method or one mode of motivation is not effective. Each social style has specific needs in regard to following a leader. Listed below are some of the needs that each social style possesses when following a leader.

Leading Analyticals

Analyticals need reasons why they should complete tasks or participate in activities. They want details and exact instruction. They need a work environment that is structured and orderly. As a leader, you need to give Analyticals space and time to think and react. They do not like to be pushed, intimidated, or manipulated. They would rather make no decision than make a bad decision.

They work well alone, but they also add value to teams by developing game plans and setting high standards. They follow through on assigned tasks and do not need leaders to breathe down their neck. They like completing tasks that require planning and accuracy, and they take their work seriously.

The Analytical social style maintains a very neat and orderly work area. Because Analyticals strive for perfection, they tend to move slowly out of carefulness and cautiousness. They like to focus and concentrate on one task at a time and do not appreciate having too many projects dumped on them at once.

Analyticals can be picky about the people with whom they work. They have a difficult time working with people who do not keep deadlines and disregard rules or regulations. They can become critical and negative concerning people who perform at low standards or produce mediocre workmanship.

Analyticals resent leaders who take costly shortcuts. They want to follow someone who thinks carefully through decisions. Analyticals want things done right the first time. They do appreciate leaders who will give them clarification and suggestions. They like alternatives for implementation. They want practical methods for projects.

Leading Drivers

Drivers are natural leaders, so they are not the easiest people to lead. They do not necessarily like taking orders, and close supervision is very stifling to a Driver. They want to know exactly what you expect of them, and they will get it done (usually before a deadline).

Drivers like to have choices and need to be allowed to choose the most successful path for reaching the goals suggested by their leader. They need to know exactly what the goal is, and then be allowed to get the job done their way, at their pace.

Drivers complete tasks very quickly and are results-oriented. They will often find shortcuts to get the job done faster. Time is money, and they do not like wasting it. Because of their fast pace, they do not always take time to listen to other people and their concerns. They have little patience with incompetence or excuses.

Drivers thrive on reaching goals and completing tasks. They are very driven at work and do not like to engage in time-wasting activities. Chitchat is annoying to the Driver. They are also annoyed by illogical or unreasonable tasks.

Drivers do not respect leaders who will not take a stand or make a decision. They usually irritate people in the workplace with their impatience, sarcasm, and insensitivity. They expect a lot of themselves and others and are not afraid to voice their opinions. Drivers are very competitive at work and like to complete tasks before anyone else. They are ambitious workers and thrive in positions of authority.

Drivers are independent and like to work alone. If put in a team environment, Drivers help to build confidence in other people. They increase productivity and speed, and they set an example of hard work and determination.

Leading Amiables

Amiables are more concerned with people than projects. They need leaders who will work closely with them. They need assurance that they will not be left alone to complete tasks. Amiables need leaders who will not treat them harshly and will be kind and considerate. They also need leaders who will provide a tremendous amount of direction. They do not like to let their leaders down.

Amiables do not like relationship tension at work and need to be reassured that everything is all right. Leaders need to show sincere appreciation to the Amiable. Amiables like to work on teams and with people and do not work well alone. When put in a team environment, they build team spirit and increase cooperation. They inspire a positive attitude and encourage people to work together.

They do not appreciate leaders who come on too strong. Shouting or showing of anger by the leader is very stressful for Amiables and should be avoided. Too much pressure on Amiables makes it difficult for them to perform. They tend to irritate their leaders with their inability to make decisions.

Amiables try to avoid getting too much attention, but still need and appreciate praise and compliments by their leaders. They usually let others take credit for things and stay in the background while someone else gets praised.

Amiables have a difficult time saying no, even when their workload is already stressful. Leaders need to be sensitive to this and make sure they are not putting Amiables under too much pressure. Amiables also need sufficient notice if they are asked to complete a task within a certain deadline.

Leading Expressives

Expressives thrive in a creative work environment that is not weighed down with rules and regulations. They work best with freedom and flexibility. They want exciting premiums or incentives for completing tasks. They like to invent new ways to do things and want the freedom to be creative.

They tend to motivate people with their constant enthusiasm. They have high aspirations for many relationships. They need endorsement and encouragement. Expressives thrive on interaction with people and do not like to work alone. When put in team environments, Expressives bring vision to the team. They also inspire others and increase the energy level of the team. They are great with brainstorming and being creative.

Expressives have a hard time being led by dull individuals who like to maintain the status quo. Expressives thrive on change and are constantly looking for ways to do things differently. While they can juggle many tasks at once, they do not always follow through. They often get bored or distracted easily and move on to new projects before completing current ones. This tends to irritate their leaders and other people with whom they work.

Expressives often jump to conclusions without having all of the facts. They make quick decisions based on a gut feeling. They also tend to make generalizations from a sampling of one. They like to take risks and expect other people to do the same.

Expressives want to feel loved and know that their contributions are appreciated. They value leaders who take an interest in their personal life. They need leaders who provide inspiration. Expressives need broad structure, but not detailed methods. They like excitement, encouragement, and personal support.

Now you know where the saying "different strokes for different folks" came from. Each of the social styles is very unique in leadership needs and in the method of working with others. As a leader, if you can learn how to lead each style, you can create a more productive, cohesive, and efficient work environment. Chart 11-B provides a summary of the important issues that need to be addressed when leading each social style.

Social Style Issues	Analyticals	Drivers	Amiables	Expressives
Motivated to save:	Face	Time	Relationships	Effort
Are irritated by:	Missed deadlines	Illogical tasks	Pressure	Rules
Irritate others with:	Negativism and criticism	Impatience and sarcasm	Indecisiveness	Lack of followthrough
Need encouragement with:	Making decisions	Listening skills	Taking risks	Checking facts
Need leaders who:	Give suggestions	Allow freedom	Provide direction	Provide inspiration
Measure progress by:	Activity	Results	Approval	Applause
Want freedom to:	Breathe	Win	Relax	Gain
Want appreciation for their:	Carefulness	Capabilities	Contributions	Cleverness
Are best rewarded with:	Private work space, systems to improve efficiency, excellence awards	Increased responsibility, leadership roles, merit raises, fringe benefits	Sincere praise and appreciation, personal gifts, acts of kindness	Flexible schedule, parties, public praise, recognition for creativity

Chart 11-B

Coping with Negative Attitudes of Annoying People

The four social styles can all have good attitudes, or they can have bad attitudes. How do you deal with their negative attitudes in the workplace? We are aware of one company that had difficulty when it came to firing employees, regardless of their social style. There was no problem in the areas of being late to work, or stealing from the employer, or fighting on the job. Those situations were easy to document. What was difficult was disciplining employees when it came to a poor attitude.

How do you document a negative attitude? It is so subjective. For this reason, the company added the following form (11-C) to its employee evaluation process. The form was designed to help clarify and objectify attitude in terms of content of words, tone of voice, and nonverbal behavior. This form can be of use in helping to identify conflict that comes in the form of what is commonly called "attitude."

Attitude in Performing the Actual Work and the Corresponding Interpersonal Relationships Involved

This is a subjective evaluation and is more difficult to document, but nevertheless is just as real. It involves the primary focus on how fellow workers and/or supervisors feel about, and whether they can work in harmony with, the evaluated individual.

Attitude is a consistent state of mind or feeling that, over a period of time, manifests itself through the content of words, tone of voice, and nonverbal behavior.

Content Of Words	Tone of Voice	Nonverbal Behavior
[ ] Put-down humor	[ ] Talking down to	[ ] Little eye contact
[ ] Pessimistic	[ ] Mimicking	[ ] Walking away
[ ] Angry	[ ] Whining	[ ] Ignoring
[ ] Hostile	[ ] Argumentative	[ ] Hand and finger signs
[ ] Rude	[ ] Defensive	[ ] Silent, angry stare
[ ] Sarcastic	[ ] Accusing	[ ] Gritting of teeth
[ ] Lying	[ ] Yelling	[ ] Making faces
[ ] Bitter	[ ] Attacking	[ ] Throwing things
[ ] Negative	[ ] Grumpy	[ ] Folding arms
[ ] Gossip	[ ] Grouchy	[ ] Pouting
[ ] Slander	[ ] Impatient	[ ] Tears
[ ] Divisive	[ ] Angry, cross	[ ] Yawning
[ ] Critical	[ ] Testy, catty	[ ] Raised eyebrows
[ ] Irritated	[ ] Sighs, grunts	[ ] Frowns
[ ] Spiteful	[ ] Exasperated	[ ] Angry looks

Chart 11-C

12

How to Follow Annoying People

Every great person has first learned how to obey,
whom to obey, and when to obey.
—WILLIAM WARD

———

I just got transferred to Joan's department. She is one hard-nosed woman! She keeps piling the work on me like I am some sort of assembly line. She certainly gets a lot done. I get exhausted just watching her. I have to admit that I do appreciate the way she keeps the team on track and focused, though. I didn't have that with Brett." Jeff was giving Barbara an earful.

"Well, I think I prefer Brett's laid-back style to Joan's autocratic style. Brett doesn't ride us all the time and is very easy to get along with. He cares about his people and makes us feel like we are part of the team. Our projects do seem to take longer, though, because he has a tough time making decisions. I guess you have to take the good with the bad." Barbara got another cup of coffee and went back to her desk.

Learning how to follow someone with a different social style can be a challenge. When you learn to complement your own style with the styles of other people, you will find a much more productive avenue to reaching your goals and the goals of others.

When you learn to recognize the social styles of the leaders you work with, you can learn to follow those leaders more effectively.

If you reviewed the charts containing famous social styles in chapter 8, you observed an interesting fact. You will find all four social styles in a variety of leadership positions. Each social style has its unique characteristics when it comes to leadership. An overview of social styles is covered below, plus what you can expect from each as a leader. There are also some practical tools for adapting to each leadership style.

Following the Analytical

Analyticals are the technique specialists. They excel in establishing policies, schedules, routines, and procedures. They can handle enormous amounts of details simultaneously. Analytical leaders are generally appreciated for their dependability. They are responsible, persevering, and accurate. They fulfill obligations and keep their promises and commitments.

Analytical leaders are often seen as very professional and self-disciplined. They possess the ability to approach decisions both logically and carefully. They tend to preserve the traditions of an organization and avoid taking risks that could negatively affect the company.

When Analytical leaders are having bad days, they have the tendency to stir up negative feelings in those who work under them (very frustrating for the Amiable and Expressive). They can also overload a person with facts, which completely annoys the Driver and Expressive.

Data collection and analysis can become such a strong focus for the Analytical that important decisions may be put off or not addressed. The slow pace of Analyticals is a source of contention for Drivers and Expressives.

Followers often complain that the systematic thoroughness of the Analytical turns into picky perfectionism. Followers often feel the tension of the Analytical's negative and critical thinking (which is stressful for the Amiable).

When Analyticals get involved with tasks, they often become quiet and withdrawn from interaction. They can be viewed as cool, distant, reserved, or aloof. Followers dislike their lack of warmth, stern commands, and austere actions. They are also seen at times as stuffy and unable to have fun or enjoy close relationships (which is an irritant for the Amiables and Expressives). Analyticals are resistant to change and can throw cold water on new ideas, frustrating Expressives and Drivers.

Tips for Following Analyticals	
✦ Stay organized	✦ Do not initiate unapproved change
✦ Keep good records	✦ Stay more formal and businesslike
✦ Provide lots of details	
✦ Present a list of things that could go wrong	✦ Follow their policies
✦ Allow them to vent the negative before a decision is made	✦ Talk soft and slow
	✦ Do not come on too strong
✦ Allow them time to think through decisions	✦ Finish what you start
✦ Do not make rash decisions	✦ Show that you take your responsibilities seriously
✦ Get all of the facts correct	✦ Double-check your work for accuracy
✦ Use good manners	✦ Do not pop into their office unannounced
✦ Listen attentively to all of their facts	
✦ Do not display impatience	✦ Keep work areas neat and tidy
✦ Do not exaggerate	✦ Have a method for your work
✦ Compliment them for their planning abilites	

Chart 12-A

If you are in a position where you have an Analytical as a leader, there are some ways you can adapt to meet that style of leadership and create a more cohesive working relationship. Chart 12-A provides general tips for following Analytical leaders.

Following the Driver

Drivers are the control specialists. They excel in taking initiative, getting things done, and making decisions. Driver leaders manage by objective and do not engage in micromanagement.

They are not concerned with details and prefer to evaluate the end result. They usually allow followers a good deal of independence to get their jobs done.

Drivers are visionary leaders who inspire followers to rise to the challenges and opportunities set before them. They can easily conceptualize ideas and describe them so vividly that followers can visualize the end result. Drivers make decisions quickly and easily and would rather make a bad decision than make no decision at all. They are willing to take risks, and their work environment moves at a very fast pace.

The implications of decisions and problems are easily understood by Driver leaders. They love complex situations and shoot for lofty goals. They are very efficient, productive, and they serve as change agents in the organization.

Drivers can become human tornadoes when things are not going as they would like them to. They can become bossy, stubborn, and demanding (a source of contention for the Amiables and Analyticals). They may make hasty decisions that get them into trouble.

Drivers have a tendency to take on large and complex problems, push them to a certain point, and then pass them on to someone else. They do not like to maintain what they start. Drivers often appear restless and unfulfilled.

They are often viewed as cold as ice and as unfeeling as a piece of steel. Amiables and Expressives especially feel put off by Drivers. The leadership style of Drivers is often tough and sarcastic. They become impatient when they have to repeat directives to the troops, and they loathe laziness and frivolity on the job. They dislike chitchat and small talk, which annoys the Expressives and Amiables. Drivers have little sympathy for those who complain that they are too demanding or overwhelming.

If you are in a position where you have a Driver as a leader, there are some ways you can adapt to meet this style of leadership and create a more cohesive working relationship. Chart 12-B provides general tips for following Driver leaders.

Tips for Following Drivers

✦ Pick up your pace	✦ Do not be irresponsible
✦ Avoid small talk	✦ Do not whine about the workload
✦ Do not interrupt their work	✦ Be active
✦ Stay businesslike	✦ Look busy
✦ Stay calm	✦ Do not be lazy
✦ Do not make excuses	✦ Do not take their sarcasm personally
✦ Get things done ahead of deadlines	✦ Make decisions
✦ Do not overwhelm them with facts or details	✦ Do not expect them to supervise you closely
✦ Do what you say you will do	✦ Toughen up around them
✦ Do not expect them to hold your hand	✦ Do not expect sympathy
✦ Display independence	✦ Take responsibility
✦ Get back to them quickly	✦ Solve problems
✦ Do not procrastinate	✦ Avoid arguing with them
✦ Do not beat around the bush	✦ Do not be wishy-washy
✦ Get to the point	✦ Do not get emotional

Chart 12-B

Following the Amiable

Amiables are the support specialists. They excel in getting along with people and making them feel comfortable. Amiables are friendly and cooperative in their contact with employees, administrative staff, vendors, and just about everyone with whom they come in contact. They are diplomatic in their dealings with people and make great spokespersons for their organizations.

Amiables are very patient and great listeners. They can be generous to a fault. They provide sincere appreciation and positive feedback to their followers. Amiables are always willing to help and be team players. They have a supportive, easygoing nature that followers appreciate.

They can also be so nice that it is difficult for followers to get angry with them, even when frustration arises. They can sometimes be very quiet, shy, and retiring. They may even appear apathetic and unconcerned at times.

They hate any form of conflict and will often avoid disciplining subordinates for misbehavior. Amiable leaders especially have a difficult time terminating an employee, even when the employee has become a burden to the entire organization. Amiables will put off dealing with conflict as long as possible, which is a major source of contention for Drivers and Expressives.

Because of their inability to say no, Amiables often take on too many responsibilities and become overly tired. They put off making decisions that may offend people. They tend to blame the failures of others on themselves. Amiables do not adjust well to change and hate surprises. They prefer the traditional and the predictable.

While Amiables make very diplomatic leaders, they often frustrate the other social styles with their apathetic approach to dealing with conflict. Other social styles often feel as if the Amiable leader is sweeping everything under the rug, instead of facing the issues and making decisions. Amiables worry about severing relationships and will avoid dealing with important conflict issues.

If you are in a position where you have an Amiable as a leader, there are some ways you can adapt to meet this style of leadership and create a more cohesive working relationship. Chart 12-C provides general tips for following Amiable leaders.

Tips for Following Amiables

✦ Use tact	✦ Do not be brash
✦ Be friendly around them	✦ Be encouraging
✦ Show interest in their values	✦ Do not argue with them in front of people
✦ Be diplomatic	✦ Do not criticize them in front of people
✦ Do not be rude	✦ Choose your words carefully
✦ Be respectful	
✦ Show kindness	✦ Speak softly
✦ Allow them to help you	✦ Do not pressure them
✦ Be gentle	✦ Be sensitive to their feelings
✦ Do not push them	
✦ Share your ideas nicely	✦ Give them input
✦ Tell them you appreciate them	✦ Display commitment
	✦ Do not make demands, make requests
✦ Show cooperation	
✦ Be a team player	✦ Help diffuse conflict and crisis
✦ Do not make unnecessary changes	
	✦ Do not surprise them
✦ Ask for their counsel	✦ Show your support

Chart 12-C

Following the Expressive

Expressives are the social specialists. They excel in generating enthusiasm and vision in the organization. They look for and create excitement and challenge in the workplace. Expressives always seem to be up and rarely have down days. Followers appreciate their friendly, warm, and caring disposition.

Expressives are optimistic and cheerful and have the ability to verbalize sincere appreciation for subordinates. They are spontaneous, talkative, and personable. They have a great flair for the dramatic and imaginative. Expressives are flashy, persuasive, competitive, and fun-loving.

The ability to troubleshoot in crisis is an area of strength for the Expressive leaders. They know how to get people to work together and they have the persuasive power to stimulate action.

The irritating characteristics of Expressives can create tension for followers. They can be loud, obnoxious, and downright insulting. If they are displeased with something, they will let everyone within earshot know about it. They can also be highly emotional, impulsive, and excitable, which can frustrate the Drivers, Amiables, and Analyticals.

They sometimes show up late for meetings (which is very annoying for Drivers and Analyticals), and have been known to forget important appointments. Expressives often keep people waiting, and it does not seem to bother them. They will often make commitments to themselves and other people that they do not keep.

Expressives can be very impatient leaders and become rigid when crossed. They tend to be restless and start far more tasks than they ever complete. They become easily bored and tend to switch to more exciting projects, leaving subordinates to pick up the pieces. They will even create crisis at times just to have something to do. They despise paperwork and rules. Expressives put off unpleasant tasks for as long as possible, which annoys the Drivers and Analyticals.

If you are in a position where you have an Expressive as a leader, there are some ways you can adapt to meet this style of leadership and create a more cohesive working relationship. Chart 12-D provides general tips for following Expressive leaders.

Tips for Following Expressives	
✦ Be flexible	✦ Be inventive
✦ Do not push rules in their face	✦ Embrace change
✦ Do not take their emotional outbursts personally	✦ Deal with the chaos they create
✦ Do not bore them with details	✦ Do not expect them to follow up with you
✦ Be informal	✦ Adapt to their constant direction changes
✦ Talk faster	✦ Help them with organization
✦ Try new things	✦ Do not be a downer around them
✦ Share in their excitement	✦ Praise them publicly
✦ Take risks	✦ Laugh at their jokes
✦ Be adventurous	✦ Learn to juggle many tasks
✦ Don't get overwhelmed by them	✦ Focus on the big picture
✦ Be original	✦ Acknowledge their accomplishments
✦ Socialize with them	
✦ Show excitement	

Chart 12-D

As you can see, each social style possesses very different and specific characteristics when it comes to leadership. Being a follower of each social style is a specific challenge for every other style. Drivers will struggle with different issues than Amiables, just as Analyticals will become frustrated over different issues than Expressives.

The key is learning how to adapt to each style to create a cooperative work environment. Part II will directly address more techniques for adapting to each style to prevent and reduce conflict.

13

Selling to Annoying People

There are two kinds of people in the world:
those who walk into a room and say, "There you are,"
and those who say, "Here I am!"
—Abigail Van Buren

—————

Maybe I should leave you two alone for a minute." The salesman pushed his chair back and stood up. "I'll just go grab a glass of water. I'll be back in a few minutes."

Sean and Lorraine had just finished listening to three hours of information on a time-share condo in Mexico. Sean tried to reason with Lorraine. "Look, honey, this is just too much, too fast. We need to think on it overnight and talk about all of the issues."

"What is there left to talk about? We have the money. We come to Mexico twice a year. It's exactly what we wanted, and the price is right! If we don't do it now, the deal won't be there for us later. You heard the man. We have to make a decision today." Lorraine was getting frustrated with Sean's indecision.

"Well, that's exactly what I don't like. He's just too pushy, and I won't be controlled or manipulated into making a decision. We just don't have enough information yet. If he can't sit on the deal overnight, then we need to just walk." Sean crossed his arms over his chest and leaned back in his chair.

Lorraine leaned in closer to him and started a loud whisper. "Look, you're just being stubborn. He's a nice man, and I have a good feeling about him and this deal. He seems sincere, and this is really what we wanted. It would be ridiculous to walk away now after all the time we have invested."

Just as she finished her sentence, the salesman returned. "So, would you like me to start the paperwork so we can get you into your dream condo?" Sean and Lorraine spoke at the same time but gave conflicting answers.

If you have ever had to pitch an idea, product, or service, you know that people do not all respond the same. Some people seem standoffish and want a plethora of facts. Some want to talk about anything and everything unrelated to the idea or product. Some barely let you get halfway through the presentation before they bluntly state their decision. Some refuse to make a decision without the input of other people.

When you examine the buying patterns of people in general, you will see a very clear trend among the social styles. If you are attempting to sell or pitch anything to someone, knowing the social style of that person will take you far in your efforts. Each style has a distinct way of processing information and making decisions. Your approach should be varied based on the social style of the person to whom you are selling.

Selling to Analyticals

Analyticals are the most critical of what you have to say or sell. They require a tremendous amount of facts and information. They despise exaggerated claims, and they expect you to have all the facts and data to back up any claims you make. Analyticals will usually do their own research to validate your information and need to be given the time to be comfortable with their buying decision.

People who come on too strong and are too loud will turn off the Analytical. Present your case or information slowly and quietly. They become frustrated with people who talk too fast and fly through the details. Stop and ask them frequently if they have any questions or concerns.

Analyticals are fairly private people and do not like to be asked very personal questions. Stay businesslike and do not pry into their personal lives. Do not make extended eye contact with them, as they will feel as if you are staring or invading.

Stress the quality of your idea or product and its excellence. Analyticals will look for quality flaws. They dislike generalities, so be specific in your descriptions. Expect a fair amount of negativism and criticism. They are motivated to save face. They do not want to be seen as someone making a bad buying decision. They also want to save money and will shop around for the best price.

The worst mistake you can make when selling to Analyticals is to push them for a decision. They usually want at least 24 hours to think about a buying decision, especially on a big-ticket item. Use logical persuasion and do not fight with them or contradict them. If you push them, you risk losing the sale altogether, as they would rather make no decision than make a bad one. Analyticals make buying decisions based on facts and logical information. Chart 13-A lists the general dos and don'ts of selling to Analyticals.

Dos and Don'ts of Selling to Analyticals	
Dos	**Don'ts**
✦ Provide lots of facts	✦ Come on too strong
✦ Give an organized pitch	✦ Exaggerate
✦ Use logical persuasion	✦ Push them to buy
✦ Talk softly	✦ Talk loudly
✦ Talk slowly	✦ Get personal
✦ Be specific	✦ Overwhelm them
✦ Stress quality	✦ Fight with them
✦ Allow time for questions	✦ Stare them down
✦ Validate their own research	✦ Be disorganized
	✦ Discredit their information

Chart 13-A

Selling to Drivers

Drivers are the fastest decision-makers. They will make a decision based on intuition. They do not need a tremendous amount of fact or detail. As you make your pitch to them, they will process the information rapidly and make a decision quickly.

They are usually in a hurry and do not appreciate long and drawn-out sales pitches. Probably the number-one thought in the back of a Driver's mind is "Get to the point!" If frustrated enough, they will even verbalize it. They are motivated to save time, and they will be looking at how your idea or product will save time and increase efficiency. They are not the best listeners, so the faster you make your point, the better.

Drivers really hate chitchat, so avoid small talk with them. There is the old sales saying, "People don't care how much you know until they know how much you care." This does not apply to Drivers! They really do not care how much you know or how much you care. They just want to know how your idea or product will save them time and allow them to get more things done.

They will respect someone who makes their pitch with confidence and brevity. Drivers do not like being pressured by someone to buy something, because they want to stay in control. They will walk away completely if they feel they are being overpowered, even if they want your product. Do not try to argue with a Driver. They excel in this area and will usually not give up until they win. Chart 13-B lists the general dos and don'ts of selling to Drivers.

Dos and Don'ts of Selling to Drivers	
Dos	**Don'ts**
✦ Get to the point	✦ Try to overpower them
✦ Let them stay in control	✦ Chitchat
✦ Stay businesslike	✦ Belabor your points
✦ Make your presentation quickly	✦ Pressure them
✦ Think fast	✦ Go off on tangents
✦ Be brief	✦ Talk about your personal life
✦ Show confidence	✦ Be passive
✦ Ask their opinion	✦ Argue with them

Chart 13-B

Selling to Amiables

Amiables do not like to make waves. They will often buy something they do not need to spare the feelings of the salesperson. They smile a lot, nod, and appear to be in agreement, when on the inside they may be stressing about the buying decision.

Amiables are motivated to save relationships. They will not make a buying decision that may negatively affect someone else.

They usually want to check with people who are important to them to make sure they are making the right decision. They also do not want to offend the salesperson, so they may experience major stress when asked for a decision.

Amiables prefer to have someone with them when making a buying decision, especially on a big-ticket item. They will listen attentively for long periods of time. Amiables despise rudeness and pressure. A hurried pace will also stress them out. Presentations should be made slowly and softly. Amiables do not appreciate someone who is overly loud and obnoxious.

They want a low-stress environment and do not like experiencing a negative attitude from people. The sales saying, "People don't care how much you know until they know how much you care," does apply to Amiables. They do want to know that you care about them. Stay positive in your presentation, and let them know how their buying decision will positively affect the relationships in their lives. Chart 13-C lists the general dos and don'ts of selling to Amiables.

Dos and Don'ts of Selling to Amiables	
Dos	**Don'ts**
✦ Show kindness	✦ Talk loudly
✦ Be friendly	✦ Put down their opinions
✦ Make them feel valued	✦ Be insensitive
✦ Display patience	✦ Be sarcastic
✦ Treat them gently	✦ Rush them
✦ Listen to them	✦ Pressure them for a buying decision
✦ Empathize with their concerns	✦ Overwhelm them
✦ Stay relaxed	✦ Show impatience
✦ Smile	✦ Become stressed

Chart 13-C

Selling to Expressives

Expressives love to shop, buy, listen to presentations, and do whatever else comes their way. Anything that involves other people or interaction is exciting for Expressives. They normally make buying decisions based on impulse and the gut feeling they get from the salesperson. They want to get to know the person and vice versa. They like small talk and chitchat and will often go off on tangents during a presentation.

Expressives are not too interested in massive detail. They do like to be an active part of the selling process, offering their own opinions and experiences. They will talk on and on and, if they get a good feeling about the person, they may buy impulsively. They believe that you only live life once, so what the heck!

A more vivid and colorful presentation will excite Expressives. They get bored easily and dislike the mundane. A creative approach to selling is the most effective with the Expressive personality. They also prefer informal presentations and go stir-crazy when asked to sit quietly and just listen for long periods of time.

Expressives will often need a little help to keep them focused. They are undisciplined about time and do not keep a tight rein on how long they have been talking. They appreciate people with a good sense of humor who do not take themselves or life too seriously.

Expressives are motivated to save effort. Present your product or idea in a way that shows them how they can achieve something. Explain how their buying decision will add more adventure, fun, and excitement to their lives. Chart 13-D lists the general dos and don'ts of selling to Expressives.

Dos and Don'ts of Selling to Expressives	
Dos	**Don'ts**
✦ Socialize with them	✦ Talk slow
✦ Joke around with them	✦ Be so serious
✦ Be informal	✦ Bore them with details
✦ Make a colorful presentation	✦ Neglect them
✦ Add excitement	✦ Stay businesslike
✦ Make it fun	✦ Be stuffy
✦ Ask about their personal life	✦ Ignore them
✦ Ask about their interests	✦ Be blasé
	✦ Be impersonal
	✦ Cut them short

Chart 13-D

Every social style is different, and every social style makes buying decisions based primarily on personality. Other factors may weigh in, such as upbringing and learned patterns of behavior. When attempting to sell to each social style, take the time to adapt to meet specific needs. You can ascertain the different social styles simply by observing behavior.

If you find yourself having to sell to different people, take the time to review the characteristics of each social style. Before long, you will be able to peg each person within a few minutes of observing specific behavior and mannerisms. The more you use these techniques, the easier it gets.

14

The Compatibility of Annoying People

A relationship is a living thing. It needs and benefits from the same attention to detail that an artist lavishes on his art.

—DAVID VISCOTT

———

Maybe I should ask to be transferred to a different department—better yet, a different location!" Dave was venting to his wife about one of his coworkers. "We have nothing in common, and we constantly rub each other the wrong way. Brad moves too slowly, he won't make decisions, and he never stands up to anyone. He's always complaining about me being insensitive and brash, but I just tell it like it is. If he can't run with the big dogs, maybe he should stay on the porch!"

Dave's wife smiled and offered her own thoughts. "Well, I can see where that would be frustrating for you. It's definitely a personality conflict, but I don't know if transferring is the answer. Maybe there's a way you can benefit from each other's differences. I work with Alan, and he's someone who thinks through things much more thoroughly than I do. This seems to balance out my impulsiveness. He certainly gets on my nerves at times, but I am trying to use his strengths to complement my weak areas."

Dave frowned and continued on his rampage. "Well, you obviously don't know Brad! He has no strengths! He's just weak all the way around."

"Maybe you should give him a chance, honey."

"Maybe you should spend the day with Brad, and you would understand what I mean. We butt heads on everything. It's not just me." Dave huffed and left the room.

You have probably noticed that you hit it off better with some people than others. Maybe you do not initially notice, but once you get yourself into a longer-term relationship (whether work or personal), you start to notice incompatibilities and major irritants with some people. With others, you seem to have much in common, and you notice that you think alike most of the time.

Compatibility issues exist within the four basic social styles. Some of the styles are more compatible. Some have absolutely nothing in common and seem to conflict the most. The two major areas of compatibility or tension are pace and priority.

Pace refers to the ask and tell characteristics of each style. Askers tend to think, move, and decide slower. Tellers tend to think, move, and decide faster. Askers always seem to be in slow gear, while tellers seem to be in overdrive. This area of pace will serve as a source of compatibility and tension.

The area of priority refers to the characteristics of task-oriented individuals and relationship-oriented individuals. Task-oriented people place work, projects, and things that need to be done as major priorities. Relationship-oriented individuals place people, events, and socializing as major priorities.

Analytical Compatibility

Analyticals are most compatible with Drivers and Amiables. Analyticals and Drivers are both task-oriented, so they share a common priority. They both focus on getting things done and are not overly emotional. They both value logic over sentiment and prefer facts above feelings.

Analyticals and Amiables are both askers, so they share the slow-pace commonality. They are less assertive by nature, more introverted, and more patient. Both Analyticals and Amiables will make slow and careful decisions.

Driver Compatibility

Drivers are most compatible with the Analytical and Expressive social styles. Drivers and Analyticals are both task-oriented, so they share the common priorities of work, projects, and things. Drivers and Expressives are both tellers, so they share the fast-pace commonality. They are more assertive, more extroverted, and more impatient than the Amiables and Analyticals. Both the Driver and the Expressive will make quick decisions and dislike details.

Amiable Compatibility

Amiables are most compatible with the Analyticals and Expressives. Amiables and Analyticals are both askers, so they share the commonality of slow pace. Amiables and Expressives are relationship-oriented, so they share the common priorities of people, events, and socializing. Both the Amiable and the Expressive prefer feelings to facts, value sentiment above logic, and are more emotional than task-oriented individuals.

Expressive Compatibility

Expressives are most compatible with Drivers and Amiables. Expressives and Drivers are both tellers, so they share the commonality of fast pace. Expressives and Amiables are relationship-oriented, so they share that common priority. Both Amiables and Expressives are more sympathetic and feelings-oriented than Drivers and Analyticals.

Each social style can share something in common with two of the other styles. Chart 14-A summarizes the most compatible social-style combinations.

Social-Style Compatibility	
Analyticals	**Drivers**
Are most compatible with: Drivers Amiables	Are most compatible with: Expressives Analyticals
Amiables	**Expressives**
Are most compatible with: Analyticals Expressives	Are most compatible with: Amiables Drivers

Chart 14-A

Areas of tension

In addition to the compatibility areas, each social style will also have areas of tension with the other social styles. These areas of tension are raised in the exact same areas of compatibility: pace and priority.

Pace Problems

The pace problems arise between Amiables and Expressives as well as between Analyticals and Drivers. The Amiable is slow-paced, and the Expressive is fast-paced. The Expressive wants to go, go, go, and the Amiable wants to take things slow and not be rushed. The Amiable is usually under tension, wishing the Expressive would slow down, and the Expressive is usually irritated that the Amiable will not pick up the pace.

Drivers and Analyticals share pace tension as well. Drivers are fast-paced and very decisive, while Analyticals are slow-paced and very indecisive. The Driver wants things done *now,* and the Analytical wants to think through everything that *could* go wrong. The Driver often feels like the Analytical cannot get anything done because he or she prefers analysis to decision. The Analytical is often under tension, feeling as if the Driver makes too many rash decisions and does not properly think through things.

Priority Problems

Areas of priority conflict arise between the Driver and the Expressive as well as the Analytical and the Amiable. The Driver's priority is task, while the Expressive's priority is relationship. They will have tension and conflict over what they view as important in life. The Driver will often view the Expressive as controlled by emotions, while the Expressive will view the Driver, at times, as insensitive and heartless.

While the Expressive will find joy in starting projects, the Driver will find joy in finishing them. The Driver likes to be in control, and the Expressive likes to be free. Drivers may view Expressives as too social, and Expressives may view Drivers as too autocratic.

Analyticals and Amiables have tension in the area of priority as well. Analyticals are task-oriented, and Amiables are relationship-oriented. The Analytical will often view the Amiable as too apathetic and too accepting of ideas. The Amiable will often view the Analytical as too uptight and logical. While the Analytical is attempting to methodically plan projects and tasks, the Amiable is attempting to build cohesive relationships. The Amiable will tend to ignore facts in favor of feelings, while the Analytical will tend to ignore feelings in favor of facts. This creates an area of tension between the two. Chart 14-B summarizes some of the major tensions that exist between the social styles.

Areas of Tension			
Pace Problems		**Priority Problems**	
Amiables (Asker-slow) Expressives (Teller-fast)		Drivers (Task-oriented) Expressives (Relationship-oriented)	
Askers	Tellers	Task	Relationships
✦ Less assertive	✦ More assertive	✦ Values logic	✦ Values sentiment
✦ Less aggressive	✦ More aggressive	✦ Questions conclusions	✦ Accepts conclusions
✦ Slower paced	✦ Faster paced	✦ Guards emotions	✦ Unloads emotions
✦ Slow thinking process	✦ Fast thinking process	✦ Firm-minded	✦ Sympathetic
✦ Discusses facts	✦ Discusses possibilities	✦ Generally restless	✦ Generally contented
✦ High patience	✦ Low patience	✦ Likes to organize	✦ Likes to be free
✦ Low on enthusiasm	✦ High on enthusiasm	✦ Regards feelers as aimless drifters	✦ Regards thinkers as half alive
✦ Careful with details	✦ Dislikes details		
✦ Interested in ideas	✦ Interested in results		

Chart 14-B

Pace and Priority Problems—Double Trouble

There are two combinations of social styles that have nothing in common when it comes to pace and priority, and therefore end up with double trouble when it comes to tension and conflict. The first combination is the Driver and the Amiable.

The Driver is a teller and is task-oriented. The Amiable is an asker and is relationship-oriented. The two will experience tension and conflict in both pace and priority. The Driver is very fast-paced and focused on work or other projects. The Amiable is slow-paced and wants to take life easier. Relationships are much more important to the Amiable than tasks.

The Driver is very dominant and control-oriented, while the Amiable is very acquiescent and subservient. This can result in a very oppressive relationship unless both parties agree to and are comfortable with those roles.

The Driver has no problem with facing conflict head-on, while the Amiable tries to avoid it at all cost. This creates a serious area of tension between the two. The Driver will sometimes view the Amiable as a pushover, while the Amiable will often view the Driver as a bull in a china shop (though the Amiable will probably not voice that view).

The second combination of double trouble is the Analytical and the Expressive. The Analytical is an asker and is task-oriented. The Expressive is a teller and is relationship-oriented. The Analytical is usually soft-spoken and avoids flamboyancy. The Expressive is very outspoken (and often loud) and loves the outrageous. This creates a source of tension between the two. The Analytical often views the Expressive as being ruled by the moment and driven by pure emotion, while the Expressive thinks that the Analytical needs to lighten up a little and get a life (and the Expressive has no problem voicing that view quite loudly).

Analyticals sometimes feel that Expressives are careless and frivolous and do not pay attention to detail. Expressives often feel that Analyticals are far too structured and live by the letter of the law. Analyticals get offended by the abruptness and perceived rudeness of Expressives. Expressives often feels that Analyticals do not care enough about people and their feelings.

Chart 14-C depicts the pace problems that exist between social styles, as well as the priority problems (relationship problems). The double-trouble areas can be identified when pace and priority issues exist.

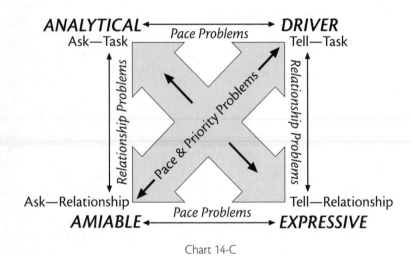

Chart 14-C

Once you are aware of the areas of potential tension and conflict, you can learn how to adjust your behavior accordingly. If you are a teller (fast-paced) and you have to deal with an asker (slow-paced), then you know that you need to slow down, talk softer, and provide more detail. Each area of pace and priority conflict can be worked out if both parties are willing to compromise on their behavior. Part II thoroughly covers conflict prevention and resolution and provides helpful tools for coping with the four annoying types of people.

Marital Issues

Marriage has to be the ultimate training ground for social-style tolerance. Many couples do not realize that much of the conflict they experience is a direct result of not understanding the potential compatibility issues and how to address the conflict.

It is not the big problems that destroy a marriage. Major tragedies like the death of a child, a house burning down, or a flood usually pull families together. It is the little things that tear relationships apart:

+ Who forgot to shut the door?

+ Who left bread crumbs on the butter dish?

+ Who is always late?

+ Who spends too much time price-shopping items?

+ Who works too much?

Individually, these behaviors are minor and silly, and none of them seems capable of destroying a marriage. But the small irritations of life are like bricks that slowly build up to form a wall, which keeps two people from knowing and loving each other fully.

The Wall

Their wedding picture mocked them from the table, these two whose minds no longer touched each other.

They lived with such a heavy barricade between them that neither battering ram of words or artilleries of touch could break it down.

Somewhere between the oldest child's first tooth and the youngest daughter's graduation, they lost each other.

Throughout the years, each slowly unraveled that tangled ball of string called self, and as they tugged at stubborn knots, each hid his searching from the other.

Sometimes she cried at night and begged the whispering darkness to tell her who she was.

He lay beside her, snoring like a hibernating bear, unaware of her winter.

Once, after they had made love, he wanted to tell her how afraid he was of dying, but, fearing to show his naked soul, he spoke instead of the beauty of her breasts.

She took a course in modern art, trying to express herself in colors splashed upon a canvas, and complained to other women about men who were insensitive.

He climbed into a tomb called "the office," wrapped his mind in a shroud of paper figures, and buried himself in customers.

Slowly, the wall between them rose, cemented by the mortar of indifference.

One day, reaching out to touch each other, they found a barrier they could not penetrate, and recoiling from the coldness of the stone, each retreated from the stranger on the other side.

For when love dies…it is not in a moment of angry battle, nor when fiery bodies lose their heart.

It lies panting…exhausted…expiring at the bottom of a wall it could not scale.

—Author unknown

Marriages often get to this point when people stop trying to understand one another. Years of annoying habits and traits wear on those who fail to learn, understand, and adapt to a spouse. While people are often attracted to someone who possesses the traits they lack, they spend years of a marriage attempting to mold the other person into their own likeness.

Having a successful marriage requires compromise. It requires two people who are willing to learn the social styles of each other and what makes each other tick. It takes two people willing to adapt their own behaviors to meet the needs of their spouses. It takes a self-sacrificing kind of love that has been clearly defined for us in 1 Corinthians:

> Love is patient, love is kind.
> It does not envy, it does not boast, it is not proud.
> It is not rude, it is not self-seeking,
> it is not easily angered, it keeps no record of wrongs.
> Love does not delight in evil but rejoices with the
> truth.
> It always protects, always trusts, always hopes,
> always perseveres.
> Love never fails.
>
> —1 Corinthians 13:4-8

Take the time to pray with your spouse and ask God to show you how to truly love *His* way. As you learn the specific social style of your spouse, commit to compromise as you learn what annoys your spouse and what your spouse truly values. As you make the necessary adjustments in your own behavior, you will find a deeper level of cohesiveness and harmony.

15

Dispelling Ten Stereotypical Gender Myths

*One of the striking differences between a cat and a lie
is that the cat has only nine lives.*
—MARK TWAIN

~~~

Men are such slobs! I spent the entire day picking up all of the junk Sal left in the conference room. His desk is always a mess, and he is the most disorganized manager I have ever seen," Betty said, as she and Sally were waiting at the fax machine for their documents to come through.

"Yeah, it's a guy thing. Tom is the same way. Yesterday I found 14 dirty paper coffee cups stacked up on the shelf behind his desk. He has yellow sticky notes all over the wall, and I don't know how he keeps anything straight. Bottom line: Men are slobs."

Meanwhile, Sal and Tom were standing in the conference room shooting wadded up pieces of paper into the corner trash can. "What is it with women?" Tom asked. "It seems like they are always nitpicking everything we do. I won't come out and call them nags, but they sure are verbally repetitive! I think they just

145

want to spoil our fun and try to keep us in line. It's a female control thing."

"It's a chick thing, no doubt," Sal agreed, as his shot hit the side of the wall and banked into the trash can. "But it's not like we can say anything about it because they will get all emotional and cry on us!" Tom started laughing as he attempted a shot over his shoulder. He missed.

There are some obvious major differences between men and women. Some people attempt to ignore or negate any differences and lump the genders into one big class. On the other hand, some people attribute differences between men and women to gender differences, when they are really social-style differences. Some of these differences have been categorized as belonging to either men or women. So when society continues to teach that women are emotional and men are not, emotional men think something is wrong with them. This next section is designed to dispel many of the gender myths that have been perpetuated by society.

Myth #1: Women Are Emotional and Men Don't Cry

This is probably the most common myth that continues to spread from generation to generation. It is a very dangerous myth as well, because it erodes the self-esteem and positive identity of those who do not fit nicely into the gender stereotype. The truth is much different than the myth.

Expressives and Amiables are more emotional by nature, while Drivers and Analyticals are not. It does not matter if they are male or female. Young Expressive and Amiable males are often labeled as "cry babies" when they display emotion. As a result, as they grow older, they may adopt conditioned behavior that suppresses the expression of those emotions. The emotional nature is still there. Expressives and Amiables are more sensitive to the feelings of other people. They believe in the free expression of feelings. The Expressive social style is just more flamboyant in the expression of emotion than the Amiable.

Expressive and Amiable males are often dubbed as being "sensitive," or in touch with their "feminine side." Hogwash! They are simply more emotional by nature and are driven more by feelings than logic. They may hide it in public or around people they do not know in order to avoid the social teasing that comes with male emotions, but the emotions are still there.

Drivers and Analyticals are less emotional by nature and are often annoyed with overemotional displays (Disclaimer: The exception would be female Drivers and Analyticals with PMS— they may show more emotion than usual as hormones fluctuate). Male Drivers and Analyticals are socially acceptable as being low on emotion. The females are often dubbed as "hard-hearted" because they do not fit the stereotypical myth of being an "emotional female."

Driver and Analytical moms tend to be less tolerant of emotional children and may say things like, "You're fine, brush yourself off," or "Stop crying before I give you something to cry about." Drivers are especially notorious for being intolerant of too much emotion.

As you can now see, it does not matter if you are male or female. The emotional aspect of your nature has more to do with your social style than your gender.

Myth #2: Men Hate Shopping and Women Love It

This is a myth that is continually supported by advertisers and society in general. The fact is, the four social styles all approach shopping a little differently, and it has nothing to do with gender.

Analyticals do not mind shopping because they like to compare prices. They will examine every item in the store and compare it to other stores. Analyticals will drive clear across town to save 20 cents on an item. They do a lot of research on big-ticket items and do not mind spending all day shopping to make sure they got the best deal and the best quality. Men are no exception to this rule. Analytical men price shop just as much as Analytical women.

Drivers do not like shopping at all. They view it as a necessary task and will get in and out as quickly as possible. Drivers often shop with a certain amount of resentment. They hate being bothered by salespeople. They want to be left alone to find what they are looking for and move on to the next task. Women are no exception. Driver women do not like to shop. They do not like to clip coupons, and they do not fit the mold that "women like to shop."

Amiables like to shop, and salespeople easily sway them. They will even buy things they do not need to avoid hurting someone's feelings. They have a hard time saying no to a pushy salesclerk. Amiables prefer to go shopping with other people, not for the shopping, but so they can spend time with them. Whether the Amiable is a male or female is irrelevant.

Expressives like to shop and buy things on impulse. They love sales, and they do not mind spending all day shopping as long as they can interact with people and have a great time. They are easily distracted and sometimes forget what it was they came shopping for. Male Expressives are no exception. They like shopping and socializing and will not fit into the stereotypical mold that "men hate to shop."

Shopping is not a gender issue; it is a social-style issue. The different social styles respond differently to the idea of shopping, whether they are male or female. So if you enjoy shopping and you are a male, go for it! If you hate shopping and you are a female, do not feel guilty about it (not that you would anyway, if you are a Driver!). Be comfortable with your unique social style.

Myth #3: Men Are More Independent and Women Are More Clingy

Society often paints a picture of men as being the independent sex, while women are portrayed as needy and clingy. Independence is more of a social-style issue than a gender issue. Drivers and Analyticals are task-oriented instead of relationship-oriented. As a result, they do not depend on relationships as much as Expressives and Amiables do.

Drivers and Analyticals tend to receive a fair amount of fulfillment from projects and tasks. Driver and Analytical women are not clingy and needy and are often viewed as very independent (especially Drivers). This independent nature is visible in male and female Drivers and Analyticals. Gender is not the driving force; social style is.

Expressives and Amiables are much more relationship-oriented than task-oriented. As a result, they often depend more on relationships for fulfillment in their lives. Amiables especially tend to be more dependent, whether they are male or female. Expressives and Amiables want a lot of interaction and involvement with the people in their lives. That makes them appear needier to the Drivers and Analyticals. Again, gender is not the issue; social style is.

Myth #4: Women Like to Chitchat and Men Do Not

This is another well-known myth that is attributed to gender. Women are categorized as creatures who want to come home and have small talk all evening about their day. Men are stereotyped as creatures who want to come home and be left alone.

The truth is, it depends on a person's social style. Drivers do not like small talk, whether male or female. They want someone to get to the point. They are the ones who come home from work and prefer to be left alone for a while.

Analyticals, on the other hand, tend to belabor a point with too much detail. That is not to say that they enjoy a lot of small talk, but when they do tell a story, they give much more detail than a Driver wants to hear. Additionally, when the Driver is telling the story, the Analytical is constantly stopping him or her and asking for details that the Driver often leaves out in a rush to get to the point.

Expressives love to talk. It does not matter if the Expressive is a male or female. They want to talk about their day, everyone else's day, and what is going on in the world. They will talk to anyone who will listen. They can talk at high speeds of 200 miles per hour, with gusts up to 300. They like chitchat and love to make small talk. They will get involved in any conversation.

Amiables love to listen. They appreciate the interaction between two people and need to know that they are loved and accepted. If they spend too much time around someone who never wants to talk, they may think they did something wrong and become depressed. Again, it does not matter if the person is male or female; it is a social-style issue.

Myth #5: Women Are Neat and Clean, While Men Are Slobs

Men really get a bad rap in this area. You have probably heard it said many times (or maybe you have said it): "Men are such slobs." Some men are, but so are some women. It depends on the person's social style. Analyticals are clean freaks. They want everything in the proper place and keep a very neat and tidy work area.

They also like things picked up around the house and hate clutter. Analytical men are very neat and orderly, just as Analytical women are.

Drivers are very organized and can whip things into shape in a matter of seconds. They do not need everything to be completely in order, but they do appreciate structure and control. They like to save time, so they want things where they can find them. You will not find their work areas or houses in complete disarray.

Amiables do not place total cleanliness and organization at the very top of their priority lists. They tend to be apathetic about things like that and are often viewed by Drivers or Analyticals as being too lazy. If they feel that a mess or disorganization is bothering someone, they may rectify it just to avoid the potential conflict.

Expressives just want to have fun, and structure and an orderly environment is not fun for them. A high priority is saving effort, so if they feel the need to clean an area, tossing things in a nearby drawer or closet is a viable alternative. They have plenty of energy but would rather spend it socializing than cleaning up.

Myth #6: Men are Natural Leaders and Women Are Natural Followers

Here is another big myth that gets perpetuated by society. Any of the four social styles can function in a leadership position, but some are more natural leaders than others. Gender is not the issue here; social style is.

Drivers are natural leaders who actually have a difficult time being followers. It does not matter if they are male or female. All Drivers seem to gravitate toward leadership positions or positions of authority.

Amiables are reluctant leaders and actually prefer to follow when possible. They do not like the spotlight, and they prefer that other people receive the public recognition and praise. Amiables tend to stress about some of the difficult decisions that come with leadership positions because they do not like to step on people's toes. This is true of male or female Amiables.

Analyticals and Expressives do not mind positions of leadership, although their styles will differ greatly. Expressives prefer the leadership role if it means lots of social interaction. Analyticals, on the other hand, prefer the planning, organizing, and structure aspects of leadership. They love establishing policies and procedures but struggle with the decisiveness that is necessary in leadership. Again, it is not a gender issue, but a social-style issue.

Myth #7: Women Are Relationship-Oriented and Men Are Task-Oriented

Women are often viewed as the ones who want to curl up on the couch, sipping tea, and watching a "chick flick" with another person nearby. Men, conversely, are viewed as wanting to go out to the garage and work on the car or get some important projects done.

This carries over into the workplace as well. Women are stereotyped as being the ones who want to stand around and gossip over coffee, while men have important tasks that need to get accomplished. As with every other gender myth, it is a social-style issue and not a gender issue.

Expressives and Amiables are relationship-oriented and like doing anything that involves other people. Amiables especially like activities that involve people they know and are comfortable with. Expressives like the new and daring and will gravitate toward any activities that involve people in general. Both Amiables and

Expressives like open displays of affection. This relationship-oriented nature can be found in both male and female Expressives and Amiables.

Drivers and Analyticals are the task-oriented ones. They are usually thinking about projects that need to get done instead of relationships that need attention. They do not get all mushy over movies, and it does not matter if they are female. They are still task-oriented. They become easily annoyed with people at work who spend too much time talking and not enough time creating results or planning for the future. They are not as open and free with displays of affection as the Amiables and Expressives.

Myth #8: Women Are Creative and Men Are Dull

Women are often painted with the brush of creativity and flair. Women are viewed as the ones who like "foofy" things with lots of color and flair. Men, on the other hand, are viewed as dull and unable to appreciate the softer things in life.

Once again, it is a social-style issue. Expressives are the ones with a real flair for the creative. They have wild imaginations and love vivid color. It does not matter if they are male or female. It is in their nature. There is never a dull moment with the Expressive, whether male or female. Amiables tend to avoid drawing attention to themselves and are less flamboyant than Expressives. Amiables do enjoy sentimental things and are creative about displaying family photos and mementos. They love to give and receive handmade gifts.

Drivers appear to be the least interested in sentimental things. You will not usually find a female Driver with a "foofy" house or office. They usually prefer more power symbols than symbols of softness. Analyticals can be viewed as dull at times due to their reserved nature and soft-spoken tone. They do have great taste for quality and like customized things. Analyticals often have a creative side to them that not everyone sees. They can be very musical, poetic, and appreciative of beauty. Again, whether male or female, the social styles have unique characteristics that transcend gender stereotypes.

Myth #9: Women Are Late for Everything and Men Are on Time

Movies are notorious for stereotyping women as always being late. The man comes to pick her up for a date, and she is still putting on her makeup. The guy is trying to rush out the door, and the woman is taking her sweet time. The woman is always harried and rushing to work. Myths! All myths!

The truth is, it depends on the individual's social style. Drivers are almost never late, whether male or female. They are not necessarily overly early either. They are usually right on time or just a few minutes early. Drivers become very irritated with people who are habitually late, especially if they are kept waiting.

Analyticals are usually early. They will arrive at important meetings 15 to 20 minutes early and will be ready to go. They do not particularly appreciate people who do not take time into consideration, although they are not impatient like the Driver. Whether male or female, you will usually not have to wait on an Analytical.

Amiables are more lax about time and are usually running behind or late. They will normally apologize and feel bad as they offer an excuse for their tardiness. Their nature is more spirit-of-the-law than letter-of-the-law like the Driver and Analytical. Amiables usually will not change their behavior in this area, but will feel bad if it makes someone else upset.

Expressives are usually late like the Amiables, but they do not feel bad about it and do not offer a reason. They live very much by the spirit of the law and really do not see it as that big of a deal. They get sidetracked with talking and socializing and forget that they needed to be somewhere 15 minutes ago. Expressive males are no exception to this rule, and they will be the ones to keep a Driver female waiting.

Myth #10: Men Like to Make Decisions and Women Do Not

This is another area where movies have painted women as indecisive and men as impatient. You often see a man and a woman trying to make a buying decision, and the woman just cannot seem to make up her mind. The man is seen crossing his arms and tapping his foot, fuming with impatience. He finally bursts out with, "Would you please make up your mind?"

Well, that is just not reality. The ability to make quick decisions is determined by social style and not by gender. Drivers and Expressives are very quick decision-makers. Drivers would rather make a bad decision than no decision, and they base their decisions on intuition. They process information quickly and do not need a lot of detail. Drivers become annoyed and impatient with the social styles that are indecisive.

Expressives also decide quickly, but their decisions are usually based on impulse. They accept conclusions easily and make decisions rapidly. They can also become impatient with slow decision-makers. Whether it is a male or female Driver or Expressive, decisions will be made quickly!

Analyticals and Amiables are much more reluctant to make decisions, and they would be the ones who are told to make up their minds. The person telling them is usually a Driver or an

Expressive. Analyticals would rather make no decision than make a bad decision. They want all of the facts before they decide, and even then, they may want more time.

Amiables are fearful of making the wrong decision and being rejected for it. They hate conflict, and sometimes making a decision causes conflict. When you ask them what they want to do, they are usually the ones replying, "I don't know. What do you want to do?" Drivers especially become impatient with Amiables because they appear as if they will not take a stand. Amiables are usually the ones saying, "It's just not worth the conflict."

Again, there are many differences between men and women that can be attributed to gender. However, many of the stereotypical myths that establish differences between the sexes are not gender differences. Those differences are social-style differences and can be observed in males and females.

16

Mottos and Sayings of Annoying People

The wisdom of the wise and the experience of the ages are perpetuated by quotations.
—Benjamin Disraeli

Have you ever read ancient proverbs and wondered why some of them seem to contradict other ones? Have you ever heard wise old sayings that seem to do the same thing? For example, one saying reads, "Look before you leap," while another one says, "He who hesitates is lost." There is a good reason for this. The four social styles have been around since man has been in existence, so it only makes sense that sayings will reflect the various beliefs of the writers.

Some writers are Driver styles, some are Analytical, some are Amiable, and some are Expressive. Each social style has a very distinct way of looking at things. Some of the social styles share certain views, while other styles differ greatly.

Below are some examples of proverbs and sayings, with respective social styles that were most likely responsible. Quotes by some of our great leaders also show a distinct social style in action.

Conflicting Sayings

Look before you leap.
(Analyticals or Amiables)

He who hesitates is lost.
(Drivers or Expressives)

―――

Beware of Greeks bearing gifts.
(Drivers and Analyticals)

Never look a gift horse in the mouth.
(Expressives and Amiables)

―――

Too many cooks spoil the broth.
(Drivers and Analyticals)

Many hands make light work.
(Expressives and Amiables)

―――

Plan for the future.
(Drivers and Analyticals)

Live for today.
(Expressives and Amiables)

―――

It is better to be silent and thought a fool, than to open your mouth and remove all doubt.
(Analyticals and Amiables)

Opportunity knocks but once.
(Drivers and Expressives)

———

Nothing ventured, nothing gained.
(Drivers and Expressives)

Only fools rush in.
(Analyticals and Amiables)

———

Finding Social Styles in Famous Quotes

I love listening to great speakers. I have read many of the great speeches given by some of our famous leaders in the past. Winston Churchill, Thomas Jefferson, Abraham Lincoln, Martin Luther King Jr.—all of these men had a way with words. As I read their speeches, I could see a pattern of social style emerging from each writer. Some of our great leaders were much softer and more compassionate in their speeches, while other leaders projected more toughness and resolve. Some leaders were long-suffering, while others were immediate initiators.

Somewhere between 15 and 20 years ago, I read Dale Carnegie's book *How to Win Friends and Influence People.* After reading his book and listening to his tapes, I realized that he epitomized the classic Amiable personality. He is just the nicest guy on the face of the earth teaching everyone else to be nice. How nice.

After listening to Zig Ziglar speak, I realized that he was the classic Expressive personality. He is flamboyant, funny, animated, and always happy. He captivates audiences with his stories, and he always has something uplifting and positive to say. I cannot ever picture him fighting with "the redhead" (his wife), but I imagine she always knows where he is coming from.

When you examine the quotes and sayings of famous leaders, you can see some of the social styles emerge in their words. Small sentences and simple phrases often give away the basic social style behind the comment.

Different social styles take on different views, values, and priorities in general. It is not difficult to spot the differences when you begin to understand the concept of the four social styles. Chart 16-A gives examples of famous quotes and the type of social styles most likely to reflect such a quote.

Life Mottos of Annoying People

All people have a motto in life. They may not always voice it, but you can tell what it is by the way they live their lives. There are those who live cautiously and would rather not take risks. They approach life frugally and methodically, and they take pride in their planning. They do not speak impulsively and appreciate the real facts in life.

Then there are those people who want to achieve it all. They are often referred to as overachievers. Goals are very important to these people, and perseverance is king! They take pride in the action they continually initiate and the amount of things they accomplish. They speak what is on their mind and would appreciate it if everyone else did, too.

There are also those people who take life in stride. They believe firmly in living in harmony and would like the world to be at

Quotes of Famous Leaders

Leader Name	Quote	Social-Style Type of Quote
Winston Churchill	"Personally, I am always ready to learn, although I do not always like being taught."	Drivers and Expressives
Golda Meir	"Those who do not know how to weep with their whole heart do not know how to laugh either."	Amiables and Expressives
Theodore Roosevelt	"Get action. Seize the moment. Man was never intended to become an oyster."	Drivers and Expressives
Abraham Lincoln	"I do not think much of a man who is not wiser today than he was yesterday."	Analyticals and Drivers
Dale Carnegie	"If you want to gather honey, don't kick over the beehive."	Amiables and Analyticals
Norman Vincent Peale	"Plan your work for today and every day, and then work your plan."	Analyticals and Drivers
Thomas Jefferson	"When angry, count to ten before you speak; if very angry, one hundred."	Amiables and Analyticals
Margaret Thatcher	"To wear your heart on your sleeve isn't a very good plan; you should wear it inside, where it functions best."	Drivers and Analyticals
Albert Einstein	"I think and think for months and years. Ninety-nine times the conclusion is false. The hundredth time I am right."	Analyticals and Amiables
Walt Disney	"All our dreams can come true—if we have the courage to pursue them."	Expressives and Drivers

Chart 16-A

peace with everyone and everything. They are content to stay out of the limelight and in the background of life. They do not need to be center stage, and they do not care to take risks. They love to give of themselves and appreciate it when others do, too.

Then there are the wild ones! These people live on the edge and love adventure. Spontaneity and excitement are their bread and butter. They love everything about life and want to experience all they can. They speak their minds and speak them loudly. They love freedom and frivolity. Life is short, and they want to enjoy it to the fullest.

Each social style could have a few mottos for life that would be fitting. The boxes below show the different life mottos that each social style would be likely to adopt.

Analyticals

"Think before you speak."

"People don't plan to fail;
they fail to plan."

Drivers

"If at first you don't succeed,
try, try again."

"Action speaks louder than words."

Amiables

"Do unto others as you would have them do unto you."

"Practice random acts of kindness."

Expressives

"You only live once!"

"If you're not living on the edge, you're taking up too much room."

The next time you read a quote or a saying, try to determine the social style most likely to make a similar statement. Analyticals seem to spotlight contemplation, thinking, planning, and intelligence. Drivers tend to focus on action, goals, determination, and perseverance. Amiables narrow in on kindness, relationships, giving, and peace. Expressives seem to focus more on adventure, risk, positive attitude, and exhilaration.

When you take the philosophies of all four social styles, you can begin to see a well-rounded view of life. That is why it takes all kinds to make the world go 'round—the four styles of annoying people!

17

The Foundational Basis for the Four Social-Styles Concept

The ideas I stand for are not mine. I borrowed them
from Socrates. I swiped them from Chesterfield. I stole them
from Jesus. And I put them in a book. If you don't like
their rules, whose would you use?
—DALE CARNEGIE

The concept that the human race consists of four basic social styles is not a new one. Hippocrates originated it around 400 BC. He developed the idea that there were four basic temperaments among people: Sanguine (the Expressive), Choleric (the Driver), Melancholy (the Analytical), and Phlegmatic (the Amiable). He stressed that the elements inside the body contributed to the factor of personality.

Hippocrates had a strong medical background. His research identified important factors to determine the temperament of the four classes of people. His focus centered on things such as phlegm, blood, and bile. Most modern-day presentations regarding personality style do not address medical elements or origination reasoning.

Most presentations simply assert the existence of the four styles and an explanation of how each style operates.

Aristotle used the forces of nature to describe the correlation to human nature and behavior. Fire (warm), water (moist), earth (dry), and air (cool) were the four descriptions used to categorize personalities. In the early 1920s, psychologist Dr. Carl Jung broke ties with the Freudian camp and philosophies and began to develop his own. Many of his theories were based on his self-analysis and personal experiences. He began his personality theory with the distinction between introversion and extroversion.

Many people today identify and distinguish introversion and extroversion differently than was intended by Jung. Most people view introverts as shy and lacking in confidence, and extroverts as confident and outgoing. Jung distinguished an introvert as someone who preferred the realm of his or her internal thoughts and feelings. He defined an extrovert as someone who preferred the external realm of activities and interaction with other people.

Jung recognized that there were four basic ways to deal with the inner realm and the outer realm. Sensing is the first. Sensing involves gathering information by means of the senses. This involves perception of information over judgment.

Thinking is the second. Thinking involves gathering information and evaluating it through logical and rational means. This involves judging over perception. The third is intuiting, which involves perception, like sensing, but goes beyond the basic senses. Feeling is the fourth and involves interpreting information based on emotional response.

Every person possesses each of the four functions but operates predominately in one area, with a strong secondary area. The final two areas are less visible but still present. Jung developed 16 different personality types, which were narrowed down to the four social styles used by many different authors and psychologists. Dr. Jung's four social styles were labeled as the intuitor, the feeler, the thinker, and the sensor.

Katherine Briggs and her daughter, Isabel Briggs-Myers, developed the Myers-Briggs Type Indicator based on the theories and research of Dr. Jung. Their paper-and-pencil test consists of about 125 questions. Based on their respective answers, people are categorized into one of the 16 types.

While this has been one of the most popular tools for personality analysis in the workplace, it can be cumbersome and difficult to remember. The social-style concept developed by David Merrill and Roger Reid simplified the behavior theories developed by Carl Jung. The basic theories and concepts remain the same. It is just a simplified way to learn the four social styles and apply the information to everyday living.

Nearly all personality presentations are based on the four social styles or personality-type theory. Some refer to this as a temperament theory. It all boils down to the same concepts and research that originated with Hippocrates and were subsequently expanded by Dr. Jung.

Different individuals have adopted the foundational research and used the basic concepts of understanding behavior for a variety of reasons. The information has been used to improve sales, develop more effective leaders, facilitate better communication, reduce conflict, and improve relationships.

Chart 17-A reveals the variety of terms that have been commonly used in the business world to describe the same four basic social styles. As you can see from the chart, while the four social styles may be given different names, the characteristics of each style and the behavioral tendencies remain the same.

System Comparison

System	High Relationship, More Talk	High Task, More Talk	High Task, More Ask	High Relationship, More Ask
Four Temperament Theory—Hippocrates, O. Hallesby, LaHaye	Sanguine	Choleric	Melancholy	Phlegmatic
Jay Hall	Synergistic	Win-lose	Yield-lose	Lose-leave
William Marston	Inducement of others	Dominance	Steadiness	Compliance
Donald T. Simpson	Integration	Power	Suppression	Denial
Stuart Atkins	Adapting-dealing	Controlling-talking	Supporting-giving	Conserving-holding
Bill Sloan	Feelers	Sensors	Intuitors	Thinkers
Adickies	Dogmatic	Agnostic	Innovative	Traditional
Thomas-Kilmann	Collaborating	Competing	Accommodating	Avoiding
Robert E. Lefton	Dominant-warm	Dominant-hostile	Submissive-hostile	Submissive-warm
Theodore Levitt	Perceptive Thinkers	Intuitive Thinkers	Systematic Thinkers	Receptive Thinkers
Spranger	Artistic	Theoretic	Religious	Economic
Keirsey-Bates	Dionysian	Promethean	Epimethean	Apollonian
Myers-Briggs	Perceptive types	Intuitive types	Sensing types	Judging types
David Kolb	Accommodator	Converger	Assimilator	Diverger
Kahler	Rebel	Workaholic	Dreamer	Reactor
David W. Merrill and Robert H. Reid	Expressive	Driver	Analytical	Amiable

Chart 17-A

The purpose of learning and understanding the four different social styles is adaptation. The basic concept has been around for hundreds of years, yet the benefits are rarely reaped in organizations and in the lives of individuals. It really does not matter which system you use to familiarize yourself with the four basic styles. What is more important is actually using the information to increase the quality of your life.

Unfortunately, many people "dabble" in the information, but few truly apply it. The reason this book focused on the Merrill and Reid system was the simplicity. If the concepts can be made simple and easy to remember, the likelihood of application is much higher. If you have ever taken one of the more comprehensive personality analyses, chances are that you probably do not remember your exact results. Additionally, the only way you will be able to ascertain the styles of other people would be to have them take a similar comprehensive test.

With the system covered in this book, once you discover your social style, it is easy to remember (Analytical, Driver, Amiable, or Expressive). It is also quite easy to determine the styles of other people and remember some of the key behavior traits you can expect from them.

What you will want to avoid is the potential misuse of the social-styles concept. The concept has been misused when people use it for name-calling: "You're a Driver—you just run over people." "You're an Expressive—just one big mouth." "You're an Analytical—you think you know everything," or "You're an Amiable—you're just lazy." People who do name-calling will usually do that with any system that is handy.

Social styles are also misused when they become an excuse for negative behavior. I may say, "I know I was too harsh, but I'm a

Driver, and that's just how I am," as if my social style gives me a license to hurt other people.

Social styles are misused when they become a tool for determining or judging motives instead of behavior. For example, "She is such a perfectionist; she just wants to be judge and jury all wrapped up in one," or "He pretends to be a diplomat, but he's just kissing up." The social-styles system helps us identify, classify, and predict future behavior of other people and ourselves. It should not be used as a measuring stick for motives.

The social-style concept helps you to understand your behavior and the behavior of other people. If used properly, it will assist you in your efforts to get along better with those with whom you work and live. Part II will delve more deeply into conflict prevention and resolution. Specific techniques will be discussed for coping with the different aspects of conflict, regardless of social style. As you navigate through Part II, you will gain a deeper understanding of how different people respond to conflict and how you can diffuse that conflict.

PART II

Conflict Prevention and Resolution

18

What Is Conflict?

Peace is the skillful management of conflict.
—KENNETH BOULDING

Two old farmers had just bought farms next to each other. One of the farmer's hens wandered under the fence and into the other farmer's property. After laying an egg, she wandered back home. The farmer looked out his window and saw his hen coming back. He went out to the fence and noticed the egg. Just as he started to pick up the egg, the other farmer came to the fence, grabbed the egg, and began to walk away.

"Excuse me, that's my egg. My hen wandered over to your property and laid that egg."

"I can see that," the other farmer said. "The egg is on my property, so it's my egg now."

"I don't think so," the farmer insisted. "It's my hen, so it's my egg."

"Look, where I come from, there's only way to settle disputes. We take turns punching each other in the stomach 20 times, and the first one to say 'Uncle' has to let the other one keep the egg."

"That's fair," the farmer with the hen replied. "Let's do it." He began rolling up his sleeves while he eyeballed the other farmer.

The other farmer said, "Okay, I go first." He held the egg in one hand and proceeded to punch his neighbor 20 times in the stomach with his other hand. His neighbor groaned and grimaced with every punch but took all 20 without crying "Uncle." He took a deep breath and said, "Okay, now it's my turn." He balled up his fist and took a step forward.

The other farmer held out the egg and said, "Uncle. You can keep your stupid egg."

That is not exactly the best way to resolve conflict, but unfortunately, people do not always resolve conflict in the healthiest manner. What exactly is conflict? Daniel Webster defines it as:

1. Competitive or opposing action of incompatibilities

2. Antagonistic state or action (as of divergent ideas, interests, or persons)

3. Struggle resulting from incompatible needs, drives, wishes, or demands

4. Hostile encounter

As you read through the Bible, you will see instances of all four definitions above. Jesus conflicted with the Pharisees quite often due to opposing views and actions. When He entered the temple and turned over the tables, His actions were most likely viewed as a "hostile encounter."

Many of Paul's letters in the New Testament address conflict in the church. Paul's frustration over the conflicts is often voiced in his letters. He spent a great deal of time writing to the churches while attempting to give them direction in how to deal with conflict.

Conflict occurs for a variety of reasons, and there are many ways to address conflict with the goal of reconciliation or resolution.

You will soon discover that there are many faces to conflict and many reasons why it can occur. This chapter will walk you through the different aspects of conflict and why it arises.

The Many Faces of Conflict

Conflict is quite normal, natural, and to be expected when people live and work together. Conflict does not necessarily mean that one person or group of people is bad and the other person or group is good. It does not mean that the motivations on one side are negative, and the motivations of the other side are positive.

Conflict occurs when people care about an issue, there is disagreement over an issue, or there is some form of misunderstanding involved in the issue.

Conflict can occur when there are unclear jurisdictions of responsibilities and authority. When boundaries are fuzzy, people often wander into other people's territory. Role definitions may overlap. Job descriptions may not be outlined or followed.

Conflict can occur when two individuals or groups have the same interest in mind. They may be in need of, or struggling for, the same resources. The resources may be limited, and one individual or group will not be able to reach their goals.

Conflict can occur where there are communication barriers. There can be little or no communication taking place. This may be caused by time difficulties or the restraints of distance. The communication may simply be unclear, causing misunderstanding.

Conflict can occur when individuals or groups of people are dependent on others for the accomplishment of their tasks. They must rely on the performance of other people. If these people do not follow through, the project may be damaged, altered, or not completed.

Conflict can occur when different levels of authority are involved. When the chain of command is not followed, disruption can result. Jurisdictional disputes can create numerous disagreements. Various levels of power can create tension, fear, and anger.

Conflict can occur when decisions have to be made by a group of people. This type of discussion may demand the need for conflict-resolution skills. Each of the parties present may have different abilities in making decisions and handling disagreement productively.

Conflict can occur when there must be a consensus among the parties, and it is often difficult to get everyone in a group to agree on a subject. And if the group decides on a particular course of action, not everyone will support the action with full participation.

Conflict can occur when there is an excess of regulations. When rules are imposed, it is the natural tendency for people to rebel or resent those rules. New policies and procedures are not always received with open arms. Change is difficult for most people. It has been said that the only one who likes change is a newborn baby.

Conflict can occur due to a history of prior unresolved conflicts between the parties where the trust level may be extremely low. They may not want to commit themselves to another situation where they may be hurt or embarrassed. Broken commitments take time to overcome. The Chinese proverb says, "Trust, like fine china, once broken can be repaired...but it is never quite the same."

Conflict can occur when selfishness is involved. The unwillingness to negotiate, compromise, or work together can turn minor conflicts into war. Individuals, concerned only about their own welfare or interests, destroy family or business unity. The welfare of individuals or groups takes a backseat to one person's own selfish interests. Life then begins to revolve around the self-centered individual.

Conflict can occur when the different social styles become frustrated with the behaviors of the other social styles. Someone is not making decisions fast enough for someone else. Someone is not thinking through his or her decisions, and that causes conflict for someone else. Differences in behavior will inevitably cause conflict.

As you can see, there are many causes for conflict. There are also many perceptions about conflict. Some people see conflict as negative, while others see it as positive. Some see conflict as contradictory to biblical teachings, while other people believe conflict is an inevitable part of life that can be dealt with in a biblical manner. Past patterns of thinking, patterning, and upbringing certainly play a role in how we deal with conflict. Examine the lists that follow and evaluate your assumptions about conflict.

What Are Your Assumptions About Conflict?

In the two lists below, place checks in the boxes that most clearly represent your present view toward conflict.

The Dirty Dozen	The Baker's Dozen
❏ Anxiety	❏ Exciting
❏ Disagreement	❏ Strengthening
❏ Tension	❏ Opportunity
❏ Competition	❏ Enriching
❏ Threat	❏ Helpful
❏ Alienation	❏ Clarifying
❏ Pain	❏ Stimulating
❏ Anger	❏ Courageous

❑ Hostility
❑ Destruction
❑ Heartache
❑ War

❑ Creative
❑ Growth-producing
❑ Learning experience
❑ Building of relationship

How were you taught to deal with conflict?

Place a check by familiar phrases out of your past.

❑ Stop it.
❑ Knock it off.
❑ Act your age.
❑ Life's not fair.
❑ Don't hit girls.
❑ Just ignore them.
❑ Stop your fighting.
❑ Don't rock the boat.
❑ Be a man; fight back.
❑ Knock each other silly.
❑ You're driving me nuts.
❑ You'd better stop it or else.
❑ Pick on someone your own size.
❑ Stop that or you'll get a spanking.
❑ Good boys/girls don't act like that.
❑ Nice boys/girls don't say things like that.
❑ Don't talk to me like that, young man/lady.
❑ If you can't say anything nice, don't say anything at all.
❑ Sticks and stones may break my bones, but words will never hurt me.

Our past conditioning may be playing a large role in our conflict-resolution skills. If we have been conditioned to think that all conflict is bad and should be avoided, we will most likely avoid all confrontations. If we have been conditioned to "bite our tongues," we will most likely smile and not say what we really feel. There are many myths and misconceptions about conflict. The next chapter will address these myths as you begin to recondition your thinking in regard to conflict.

Our sinful nature may also be playing a role. We are engaged in a daily battle against the old nature as we attempt to live by the Spirit of God. If we are not fighting and dying to the old nature, we may be allowing old patterns of thinking and behavior to dictate how we face conflict on a daily basis. "The old man" may be rearing his ugly head as we fall back into our old patterns of coping based on selfishness.

> Those who live according to the sinful nature have their minds set on what that nature desires; but those who live in accordance with the Spirit have their minds set on what the Spirit desires (Romans 8:5).

Take a moment to stop and pray. Ask the Spirit of God to reveal to you the negative patterns of behavior that need to be changed as you address conflict in your life. Ask the Lord to cultivate a loving spirit in your heart as you attempt to cope with conflict.

19

Ten Myths About Conflict

A rebuke impresses a man of discernment
more than a hundred lashes a fool.
—Proverbs 17:10

When you think of the word *conflict*, what comes to mind? For some people, it is a negative situation that should always be avoided. For others, conflict is not such a bad thing and can result in healthy resolutions. There are many myths about conflict that should be addressed. Review the ten myths below and evaluate your own belief system about conflict. Have you ever found yourself embracing any of these myths?

Myth #1: All Conflict Is Bad

Many people believe that conflict is bad because emotions get aroused and issues are often left unsettled. Because these people do not like the negative feelings they are dealing with, they tend to avoid conflict. The establishing of the United States began with a conflict between freedom and tyranny. It took a conflict to end slavery. Standing up to a bully at school in an effort to end his reign of terror may be unnerving and difficult, but the result will give long-term peace.

Conflict often arises when the rights of one person or a group are violated. Accepting the violation does not settle the issue. The violation needs to be discussed and resolved, if possible. This brings about conflict that may result in positive change. Conflict can be positive:

✦ Conflict can increase the motivation of both individuals and groups to learn to get along with each other.

✦ Conflict can be responsible for increased creativity and problem-solving.

✦ Conflict can help individuals or a group draw together, seeking mutual goals.

✦ Conflict can lead to understanding and the clearing up of miscommunication.

✦ Conflict can help both individuals and groups to grow.

In the Book of Galatians, Paul describes how he opposed Peter face-to-face because, as Paul describes, Peter was clearly in the wrong. Paul was not afraid to address conflict in the church, and he often encouraged and admonished other people to do the same.

Myth #2: Conflict Damages Relationships

It is true that conflict can damage or destroy a relationship. It is also true that conflict can unify relationships when misunderstanding is cleared up. The resolving of conflict can draw individuals or groups together. Positive confrontation and conflict resolution can dissolve built-up bitterness and pave the way to cohesiveness. Unresolved conflict is what destroys relationships. Conflict handled in a constructive manner can actually enhance relationships.

Myth #3: Conflict Should Never Be Escalated

Sometimes conflict must be escalated before a resolution can be reached. The escalation of conflict is a major factor in labor-union disputes. It helps to force the issue and bring it to a point of resolution. The increase of conflict becomes so uncomfortable that the individuals or groups have to face each other. They have to work it out. The conflict itself becomes the catalyst that sets the needed change in motion.

Myth #4: All Conflict Is Just a Personality Problem

The implied concept is that if you disagree with me, there is something wrong with you. It must be something inherent in your character and personality. It also suggests that the only people who have conflicts are those with personality problems. The fact is, everyone will face conflicts or will start conflicts with other people. When personality and social-style differences enter in, they only add to the intensity of the conflict. They are not necessarily the cause of the conflict.

Myth #5: All Conflict Should Be Reduced or Avoided

It would be nice if all conflict could be reduced or avoided. It must be kept in mind that conflict is a universal human experience. Conflict is going to come our way whether we like it or not. We will continue to experience conflicts within our own personality. We will not be able to escape conflicts in relationships with other people. We will also be unable to run from conflicts caused by unforeseen accidents, illness, or acts of nature. It would be better to reduce our emotional reaction to conflict, rather than avoiding conflict (which is impossible). Let's learn healthy methods for dealing with and resolving conflict.

Myth #6: Conflict Indicates Psychological Problems

There is no question that people with psychological problems have conflicts, but so does everyone else. Those who have psychological issues are sometimes hampered to a greater extent in coping with their problems. They often do not possess the skills necessary to constructively deal with conflict. When conflict occurs, to say that the individual has psychological problems is simply a put-down technique. It places the person making the comment in a one-upmanship position. Conflict is normal between all people, not just between those with psychological problems.

Myth #7: Harmony Is Normal and Conflict Is Abnormal

This concept does not even touch the reality of life. Those who cannot or will not deal with conflict usually suggest that harmony is normal and conflict is abnormal. It is not a pleasant experience to confront anyone. When people find their anger and fear rising to the surface, it makes them uncomfortable. Rather than facing their emotions or the emotions of other people, they run away from conflict. They withdraw, avoid, and shun conflict situations or conflict-producing people. To help reinforce their fear, they suggest that harmony is normal and conflict is abnormal. This is used as a technique to get other people to conform to their way of thinking since it suggests that you must not be normal if you are involved in conflict. The truth is that harmony is possible and conflict is normal.

Myth #8: If I Ignore the Conflict, It Will Go Away

People often hold on to the misconception that if they ignore conflict long enough, it will disappear all by itself. Some people hold the view that attempting to deal with the conflict will only make it worse. As a result, some people choose to ignore conflict and assume it will go away.

When you ignore conflict, it merely grows. While people may remain silent on the outside about the conflict, they may be fuming on the inside. The conflict may be growing, along with more dissension and resentment. Ignoring conflict will not help the situation. Facing conflict and learning constructive ways to resolve conflict is much healthier than ignoring conflict.

Myth #9: Genuine Conflict Is About Facts and Not About Emotions

There are those who endeavor to separate facts from emotions in conflict situations. They suggest that only the facts are important. The implication is that emotions are not to be involved or, at the least, should not carry much weight. While it is true that conflict occurs over issues and facts, a person's behavior and emotions do play an important role. Emotions indicate the degree of importance the individual feels about the issue at hand. Emotions are the thermometer that indicates the intensity of the conflict.

Social-style differences will result in the manifestation of emotional or unemotional responses to conflict. Drivers and Analyticals tend to approach conflict on a lower emotional level than Amiables and Expressives.

Myth #10: Conflict Is a Sign That People Do Not Care

Nothing could be farther from the truth. Conflict is a sign that people *do* genuinely care. Their emotional attachment to the issues is a sign that they have deep concerns about the problem at hand. Their willingness to confront the issues, knowing that this confrontation can result in tension, shows they care.

When Jesus went head-to-head with the Pharisees on a variety of issues, it was not because He did not care; quite the contrary, He cared very much. When Jesus turned the tables over in the temple, it was not because He could care less about people and their feelings. Jesus dealt with that conflict because He cared very much about people and how they viewed the temple of God.

Take a moment and evaluate your paradigm when it comes to conflict. Do you view all conflict as bad and avoid it? Do you think that people who engage in conflict do not care? A close examination of our own belief system often gives us deeper insight into why we approach conflict the way we do. Ask God to unveil some myths that you may be embracing about conflict.

20

The Positive Power of Confrontation

Face the conflict.
To run from it will be a continual race.
—R. E. PHILLIPS

Denny's practical jokes are getting out of control. Can you talk to him about it?" Darlene was expressing her displeasure to Denny's direct supervisor, Cindy.

"Have you talked to Denny about it yet?" Cindy leaned forward and looked Darlene in the eye.

"No, I haven't, and I really don't want to confront him on this. You're his boss, so I thought it would be better coming from you." Darlene attempted to avoid Cindy's intense stare.

After a long pause, Cindy took a deep breath and began to speak. "Darlene, confrontation is not a bad thing. It will establish the boundaries you would like to see in your working relationship with Denny. Not everyone feels the way you do, so Denny may not be aware that he is offending you. If you confront Denny with honesty, integrity, and respect, I'm sure he will respond to your concern. If you confront him with the issue and he fails to respond properly, I would be happy to confront him after that."

Darlene leaned back in her chair and crossed her arms. "I just don't want to make the working environment any more uncomfortable than it is. I don't want him to make my life miserable if I confront him."

"The tension will only increase if you don't confront the situation. It won't go away on its own. Additionally, Denny is less likely to be resentful if you confront him first versus going behind his back or over his head. If you confront him and he attempts to make your life miserable, you can be assured that I will intervene." Cindy smiled and gave Darlene time to respond.

Darlene stared out the window for a few seconds before responding. "Well, I guess it's worth a try. I'll talk to him today and let you know how it goes."

Not every social style looks forward to dealing with confrontation. Some people view confrontation negatively. In some cases, people have had very negative experiences with confronting others, so they give up. In other cases, people simply do not want to face the potential tension that may come with the confrontation.

Review Chart 20-A for the most common ways people respond to conflict. How do you deal with conflict? Do you ignore it? Do you walk away and withdraw? Do you compromise and not really get to the real issue? Or do you confront the conflict and blast through to positive resolution?

Conflict is not always easy, and for some people, it is a dreaded nightmare. Below are some outstanding reasons why you should embrace confrontation with a positive mind-set.

1. Confrontation is an act of caring. The confronter is not willing for the other person to live with an internal discrepancy that may harm him or her. The confronter will not sit quietly by, watching the person walk blindly toward a cliff.

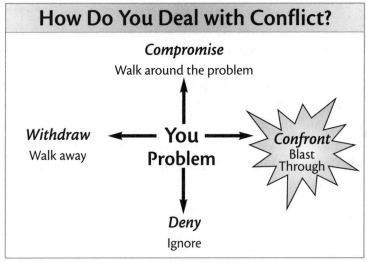

Chart 20-A

2. Confrontation is a responsibility. Confrontations we experienced with people in the past have helped us grow in wisdom and self-control. We ought to give others the same benefit.

3. Confrontation puts limits on the relationship. It states that we do not fully accept something about the other person's behavior, beliefs, or attitudes. To some extent, we reject part of the other person. This can be painful to him or her and scary for you because you wonder if you may be rejected in return.

4. Confrontation must be an act of integrity. Because entering into another person's life is risky, doing it can be motivated by selfishness—or love. The confronted person will quickly know from which motive you are acting. Confrontation must not result in dirtying the relationship with snobbery or spite. Those who confront must know the difference between punishment and discipline, right and wrong, justice and mercy.

5. Confrontation seeks to help others understand themselves better. The confronter does as much as possible to understand *before* trying to teach understanding.

6. Confrontation must be done with care and flexibility. It may take some brute force to move entrenched habits in new directions, but at the same time, confrontation needs finesse. Humans are fragile and can be painfully broken. So the confronter decides whether to be direct or indirect, to confront now or later, and whether to be gentle or tough. The vehicle of confrontation can be a limousine, a pickup truck, or a car-crushing monster truck.

7. Confrontation is an act of courage. It may strain the relationship for a time. The confronter may be ignored, rebuffed, ridiculed, attacked—or all of these. The confronter recognizes and accepts the risk and tries to keep it to a minimum.

8. Confrontation is an investment in the future. There may not be any benefit for a long time. In the short run, it is easier to avoid the hassle and not confront, but that is a second-best choice.

9. Confrontation is an uncomfortable act for many persons. Knowing that the confronted person might be a little tense often creates tension in the confronter. But avoiding or postponing the confrontation usually makes it more difficult to do later.

10. Confrontation is an act of optimism. The confronter becomes deeply involved in the life of the other person by challenging that person to become more involved in his or her own life. It is the confronter's way of saying, "Life is good. It is so good that I'm not willing for you to half-live your life." (From Richard Walter's book, *How to Say Hard Things the Easy Way,* pp. 36-37, copyright 1991. Published by Permission of Word Publishing.)

While initially it may seem difficult to confront conflict, confrontation will actually reduce the amount of conflict you must face. Chart 20-B depicts the amount of success in reducing conflict relative to the conflict intensity. If the conflict intensity is extremely low, you have concealed conflict in your life (unexpressed). Coupled with the low conflict intensity is the low productiveness of reducing the actual conflict. If the conflict intensity is high and you have unrestrained expression of conflict, you will experience the same problem—the productiveness of reducing the conflict will suffer.

Once you strike a balance with managed conflict, you will begin to confront the conflicts in your life in a positive manner. The conflict is being confronted (expressed) in a balanced manner and, as a result, the productiveness of the conflict reduction is successful.

> A man of knowledge uses words with restraint, and a man of understanding is even-tempered (Proverbs 17:27).

Chart 20-B

The Monster of Conflict

I was minding myself when the monster appeared.
He was ten steps behind me, and gaining I feared.
I thought if I shunned him, he might disappear,
But luck would not have it—his steps only neared.
I rounded the corner and closer he came,
Atrocious and frightening, shouting my name.
I thought if I shunned him, he might do the same,
But his shadow was growing; he would not be tamed.
I stopped in my steps and turned swift around.
I confronted the monster and he made not a sound.
He crumbled and shriveled and fell to the ground,
Then his crumbs blew away and not a piece could be found.

—KIMBERLY ALYN

21

Dealing with Conflict Mentally

The time to win a fight is before it starts.
—Frederick W. Lewis

―――――

It's all in your mind." Have you ever had someone say that to you? "You're making a mountain out of a molehill." How about that one? Sometimes we create or escalate a potential conflict in our own minds. We jump to conclusions or we make assumptions. As a result, conflict begins to brew inside our heads before we have a chance to rationalize the facts.

Sometimes emotions get in the way. Sometimes we allow past experiences to frame the outcome of potential conflict. Once the feelings and actual facts of the conflict are mingled in our mind, actual behaviors manifest themselves. Some of those behaviors include withdrawal, aggression, competition, debate, and problem-solving. As Chart 21-A depicts, conflict begins with circumstances, comments, or behaviors, and progresses to either agreement or defeat.

The beginning of conflict starts with the path you allow your thoughts to travel down. First and foremost, you must weigh your

Conflict

Preconflict Conditions
Behavior / Comments / Circumstances
Various Forces That Lead to Conflict

Perceived Conflict

Logical and Actual Facts
About the Conflict

Felt Conflict

Feeling of Threat/Hostility
Fear/Mistrust and Hurt

Actual Behaviors

Withdrawal
Aggression
Competition
Debate
Problem-solving

Agreement or Defeat

Picking Up the Pieces

Chart 21-A

thoughts and actions against the Word of God. "Take captive every thought to make it obedient to Christ" (2 Corinthians 10:5).

Gaining control of our thoughts is a very important step when dealing with conflict mentally. As you equip yourself with the necessary tools to deal with conflict, you will be able to transition from unproductive, defeating conflict, to productive solutions. The process of mentally dealing with conflict can be best addressed with the methods that follow.

Method #1: Get More Information Before You Respond

When a conflicting event occurs, we sometimes perceive or assume that certain things are happening when they really are not. We need to get more information to determine if the way we are feeling or thinking is based on valid reasons. We may have all of the facts. We may have misunderstood what someone said. A friend or coworker could have given us false information.

> *"He who answers before listening—that is his folly and his shame."*
> —PROVERBS 18:13

Before we lash out verbally at someone, we would do well to ask a few questions first. Questions are a great way to get more information and clarify other people's words and actions. Consider such questions as:

✦ I'm not sure I understood what you meant. Could you please explain it a little more?

✦ I get the impression that you're upset with me. Are you?

✦ I noticed you were doing _____. Could you please help me to understand why you were doing that?

✦ I may be wrong, but I feel as though there may be a problem between us. Is my perception correct?

This will pose more of a challenge for the Drivers and the Expressives than the Amiables and the Analyticals. Drivers and Expressives are tellers, and tend to say what is on their mind right away. Amiables and Analyticals are askers, and tend to pause before they speak.

As you can see by Chart 21-B, conflict interrupts an otherwise tranquil existence. We may be on cruise control in life when some form of conflict triggers a reaction. The first process in coping with the conflict is the mental response. A verbal response often follows, as well as a physical response. The mental, verbal, and physical responses can all be negative responses or positive ones, depending on the choices we exercise as we face the conflict.

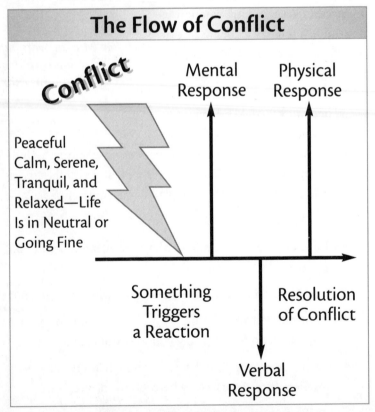

Chart 21-B

Method #2: Go to the Memory File

When you feel yourself getting upset over some conflicting event, be sure to make a stop at the memory file. Does the individual involved in the conflict remind you of someone out of your past? It could be a parent, relative, or former boss. It might be a friend, teacher, or someone in authority. The situation you may presently be facing might remind you of some previous conflict. It may be very similar. It is important not to bring feelings and emotions out of the past and add them to your present situation. As you review your memories, you may be surprised how much hurt and anger and how many old grudges you carry with you, ready to deposit on another person.

> *"The horror of that moment,"* the King went on, *"I shall never, never forget!"* *"You will though,"* the Queen said, *"if you don't make a memorandum of it."*
>
> —LEWIS CARROLL
> *ALICE IN WONDERLAND*

Method #3: Become Aware of the Displacement Response

Many of our conflict situations can find their root in our displacement of emotions. We can be upset or angry with one person and take it out on somebody else. We all have experienced having a bad day and taking out our frustrations on our family and friends.

Do you find yourself pressing harder on the gas pedal after someone cut you off on the freeway? Do you tickle your children unmercifully? Have you found yourself playing roughly with your dog? Are you short of patience? If so, you may be displacing your emotions.

Method #4: Evaluate Your Feelings

It might be very wise for you to stop for a moment and evaluate your feelings. Make some notes and list the people or things that are annoying you. Have you been hurt by something someone has said? Have you been jumping to conclusions about your situation and looking at the worst possible scenario? Are you feeling threatened or inferior? Look for patterns of recurring emotions in your life.

> *Anger is never sudden. It is born of a long, prior irritation that has ulcerated the spirit and built up an accumulation of force that results in an explosion. It follows that a fine outburst of rage is by no means a sign of a frank, direct nature.*
>
> —CESARE PAVESE

Have you ever driven down the road or stopped at a red light and noticed people talking to themselves in their cars? They are thinking about something. They are experiencing some strong emotions—strong enough to talk out loud to themselves or to the other person they are thinking about. Have you done this?

You might be wise to put your own thoughts on trial. Are they based on facts or feelings? What is the source of those thoughts or facts? Is it a reliable source? Is it biased?

As you mentally face conflict, you will experience initial feelings in response to the conflict. These initial feelings let you know there is an issue that needs to be addressed, and it is an important one. Chart 21-C shows many of the initial feelings you may experience in response to conflict.

As you examine your feelings, there are a few questions you may want to ask yourself: *Am I focusing my thinking on the positive or the negative? Am I becoming anxious, fearful, and worried? Am I trusting God or fearing the worst? Am I taking my thoughts captive to the obedience of Christ? Am I finding myself angry,*

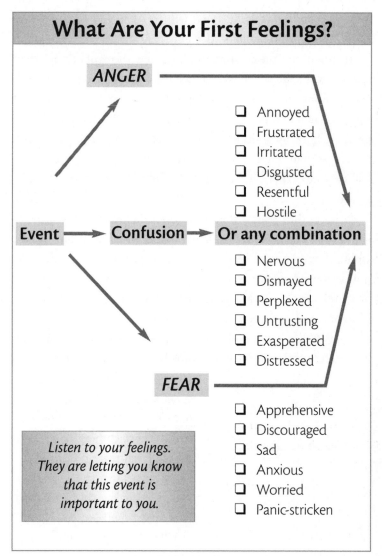

Chart 21-C

resentful, and full of hate? What will be the advantages or disadvantages of continuing to think along these lines?

It might be time to start thinking new thoughts rather than negative self-talk. When was the last time you looked for the truth and an honorable way of thinking? How often do you seek that which is right and pure? Have you developed the habit of finding positive character traits in other people? Are there things that you should be thankful for? As you begin to change your attitude, you will begin to experience peace and tranquility, even in the midst of travails.

It is good to realize that there is a difference between problems and the facts of life. Problems are situations that you have the ability to work on and change. If you have a flat tire, you can fix it. If you need an education, you can go to school. If you are out of work, you can seek employment. If you have a conflict with someone, you can attempt to work on it.

Facts of life, on the other hand, are situations over which you have no control. You have no control over the drunk driver who kills your daughter. You have no control over an earthquake that destroys your house. You have no control over coming down with cancer. It happens to the best and worst of people. In those cases, you must make peace with pain. It is not something you should get fearful of or angry over. Worry will not change a thing. Acceptance and resignation is the only course of action that will bring peace. While you may not be able to control everything that happens to you, you *can* control how you respond to it.

> *Only 10% of life is what happens to you—the other 90% is how you choose to react to it.*
>
> —CHARLES SWINDOLL

22

What Is the Issue?

Conflict is a relationship. Where there is no conflict,
there is probably no relationship.

———

A mother cannot seem to get her teenage daughter to obey the rules. The daughter rebels and does not come home when she should. The mother continues to yell at her and sends her to her room. The cycle continues, and no one seems to know how to get to the heart of the issues.

A church member is fed up and leaves the church. No one seems to listen to anything he has to say, and he feels like his ideas are constantly dismissed. The church seems to embrace stagnancy, while he longs to embrace change.

An employee hates his boss. He loathes coming to work in the morning, and his attitude is slowly worsening. His boss feels like every effort has been made to solve the problem, but he is not exactly sure what the real issue is. The employee has never taken the time to really pinpoint what the real issues are, either.

The city council meetings seem to be getting more tense every month. Conflict abounds, and the town appears to be polarized. When one group supports a project, the other group inevitably opposes it. The verbal bashings at the microphone escalate as each side states its views. As emotions escalate, everyone seems to lose sight of what the real issues are.

The nation seems to be more and more divided as each year passes. Republicans and Democrats continue to conflict over issues that are emotionally volatile and extremely heated. As the debates escalate, the real issues are often neglected as emotions rise. Each side is very passionate about its views and is willing to take a strong stand on what is important for the nation and what is not.

One country values democracy, while another maintains the value of a dictatorship. Other countries step forward with their own values, beliefs, and religion as they join in the conflict. As the conflict escalates and countries maintain their willingness to fight and die for what they value, war emerges from the conflict. Oftentimes there are more issues than one, when conflict escalates to war. Identifying all of those issues and finding agreement on what the issues really are is not always easy. Sometimes it is downright impossible.

The level of conflict you will have to face may vary from mild to extreme. Have you ever been in the midst of conflict and lost sight of what the issue really was? Maybe you were never really sure of the issue in the first place. True conflict resolution requires that we focus our attention on what the issue is and find viable solutions to the conflict.

Conflict can exist at a minor level on a minor issue, or it can exist on a large-scale level on a major issue. Conflict often falls somewhere in between as well. It is important to focus on understanding what the particular conflict is all about. This can be done by looking at five major areas of conflict in people's lives. Check one of the boxes listed below that most generally represents the conflict you are facing. As conflict moves from intrapersonal to intergroup, it becomes more severe. The conflict can become so extreme that it leads to war.

Escalating Conflict

❑ **Intrapersonal**

This area involves conflicts and personal problems that individuals have within their own lives. Examples of this would include: low self-image, shyness, pride, lack of patience, quick temper, depression, and anxiety.

❑ **Interpersonal**

This area involves conflicts between two people. It could be between husband and wife, employer and employee, parent and child, relative and relative, friend and friend, or stranger and stranger.

❑ **Small Group**

This area involves small groups of people who are at variance with each other. It could include interoffice departments, church groups, community groups, and competitors in business and educational institutions.

❑ **Large Group**

This area involves conflict with larger collections of people, such as the Republicans versus the Democrats, federal employees versus private business, and/ or labor unions. It could include states' rights versus federal laws.

❑ **Intergroup**

This area involves conflict on a grand scale. This could include one country against another country. It could be a group of countries against another group of countries.

WAR

Once you determine in which major area your conflict resides, you can now begin to focus and pinpoint the conflict. This narrows the process of finding the issue and not focusing on emotions. Are you dealing with a space conflict or a scheduling conflict? Is the conflict related to methods or procedures? Is the conflict a result of personal preferences, traditions, customs, values, or beliefs? Check one of the boxes that most represents the specific conflict(s) you are facing.

Escalating Conflict

❏ Space

This refers to an infringement of territorial space. It could include invasion of physical space, an invasion of responsibilities, or an invasion of area of supervision.

❏ Schedule

This refers to a conflict of individual schedules and deadlines between two people or between groups of people.

❏ Methods

This refers to how individual people approach the tasks before them. Not everyone works at the same pace or has the same idea as to how a task should be accomplished.

❏ Procedures

This refers to a set of established forms or methods for conducting business. There is often disagreement as to these steps and the course of action to be taken.

❏ Personal Preference

This refers to your own personal taste, style, or opinion as to how a task should be done and the time it takes. It often comes down to simply not wanting to follow what is suggested.

❏ Traditions

This refers to a body of unwritten precepts that have been time-honored within the group or organization. Violating these traditions begins to threaten the group.

❏ Customs

This refers to a long-established practice or duty carried out by individuals within a group. This habitual practice often has the force of law or censure.

❏ Values

This refers to strongly held ideals, principles, and standards that are highly prized by the individual or the group. People are willing to go to war over the things they value.

❏ Beliefs

This refers to strongly held convictions by the individual or the group. Beliefs take traditions, customs, and values to the final step. The individual or the group is willing to die for what they believe.

Fight to the Death

As you discover what the issue really is, you will also discover that there are various levels of conflict. Conflict may start as a mere difference of opinion. This can be categorized as a spat. A spat normally leads to confrontation. If escalated and unresolved, the spat can lead to a heated debate or argument. This can be categorized as a quarrel. This level of conflict often leads to division. If escalated even further and left unresolved, it can then lead to intense physical anger, which can result in an actual fight. This often results in rejection. On a large-scale level, when this further escalates to having the hostility confirmed, it leads to war, which results in ultimate separation. Chart 22-A depicts the various levels of conflict.

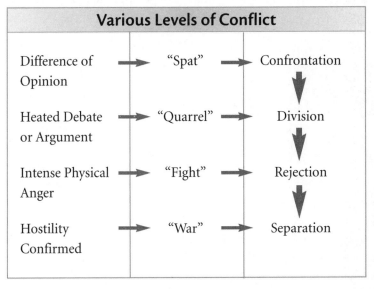

Various Levels of Conflict		
Difference of Opinion	➡ "Spat" ➡	Confrontation
Heated Debate or Argument	➡ "Quarrel" ➡	Division
Intense Physical Anger	➡ "Fight" ➡	Rejection
Hostility Confirmed	➡ "War" ➡	Separation

Chart 22-A

Once you have established and pinpointed the real issue, you can begin to take steps to resolve the conflict. Whether the conflict is merely on an interpersonal level or an intergroup level, the real issue must be examined before resolution can ensue.

Take a moment to stop and pray. Ask God to bring to your heart and mind any areas of conflict that you have been avoiding or are not dealing with in a godly manner. Ask the Spirit of God to direct you as you take the necessary steps in your life to resolve your areas of conflict. Ask for wisdom as you step out in faith and love.

The next chapter will address three broad-based basic approaches to resolving conflicts. A conflict matrix will be provided to show you how to constructively approach the conflict in your life.

23

Three Approaches to Resolving Conflict

Conflict requires energy, wisdom,
and creativity.

━━━━━━

I've had just about enough of your mouth, young man!" Patrick stood up and moved closer to his 15-year-old stepson, Jimmy. "Your constant rebellion and disrespect for your mother is going to stop, and it's going to stop now."

The conflict had been building for months. Jimmy was attempting to flex his muscles of independence, and Patrick was trying to maintain his authority in the home. The tension seemed to be getting worse, and they both felt like their backs were against the wall.

"Get out of my face. You're not my dad, and I'm sick of you trying to act like you are. How I treat my mom is none of your business!" Jimmy started to raise his voice as a red flush came over his face. His anger was mounting.

"I am the man of this house, and as long as you live here, you'll follow my rules, whether you like it or not!" Patrick poked Jimmy in the chest as he emphatically made his point. Jimmy pushed Patrick away from him and yelled, "I don't have to put up with this!" Jimmy stormed out of the house and slammed the door. Patrick was breathing hard and seething with anger. He contemplated whether he would run after Jimmy, call the police, or just let him go.

"Good morning, Joan. Have a seat." Stan motioned Joan to sit in the chair across from his desk. "How's life been treating you lately?"

"Just fine," Joan responded tentatively. She knew she had been asked into the captain's office for a reason. She could feel the "sandwich method" of discipline unfolding.

"Joan, the reason I asked to see you is because I need to discuss a matter with you. It has been brought to my attention that you played a practical joke on a firefighter here in the station. My understanding is that someone could have been hurt. I wanted to give you the opportunity to tell your side of the story."

Joan cleared her throat and began. "Well, it really wasn't that big of a deal. I rigged José's locker, and I thought he had a sense of humor. I guess I was wrong. My intention wasn't to physically harm him; it was just to play a little joke on him for all the wisecracks he makes."

"So, let me make sure I understand this. You did actually initiate the practical joke, is that correct?" Stan paused to give her time to respond.

"Yes, but it wasn't a big deal. He's been making wisecracks for way too long now!" Joan was starting to get defensive.

"Right now we're just dealing with your situation, Joan. I will address the wisecracks with José later. Do you recall a meeting we had three months ago where we discussed the rules and regs regarding practical jokes? Do you recall the conversation we had and the standard we agreed upon?"

"I remember we had a meeting about harassment and stuff like that, but I wasn't harassing José." Joan crossed her arms over her chest and leaned back in her chair.

"I have the notes here in your file from our last meeting, and they clearly define what we discussed. Please read over those notes before we continue." Stan slid the folder across the desk. Joan leaned forward and read through the file.

"I just can't see how a stupid little joke can be considered harassment." Joan did not want to admit she was wrong.

"Joan, the last time we met, we specifically discussed practical jokes in the station and why they need to be avoided. This is the second complaint I have received, and as you can see from our notes, we discussed what the ramifications would be. At this point, I am going to have to proceed with a written reprimand for your file." Stan paused and allowed Joan the opportunity to let it all sink in.

"I get it, Stan. I just really didn't think it was a big deal. I won't let it happen again. It's obvious that not everyone has a sense of humor around here."

"Joan, please understand that you are viewed as one of the best firefighters we have, and you are valued in this department. We just have to follow the regulations to reduce misunderstandings, conflicts, and accidents. I'm sure your intent was not malicious, but nonetheless, we still have to follow the rules." Stan smiled, hoping to relieve some of the tension.

"I know," Joan sighed. "I guess I just don't like all the rules and regs, but I understand why they are there. I'll keep my practical jokes at home."

Stan stood up and shook Joan's hand. "Thank you for making an effort to understand and work within the department guidelines. You're a valuable asset here." Joan shrugged her shoulders, forced a smile, and left his office.

"Look, Ben, I'm already putting in more hours than I should in my management position. When I was hired here, I agreed to work 30 hours a week. I have two kids, and I have to pay for day care. Besides, I just don't want to be away from home any more than I already am. I realize there are deadlines that need to be met, but we are just too short-staffed right now. Not only am I functioning as a manager, but I am also doing projects that should be done by team members. We just don't have enough team members to do all of the projects." Pamela was making her case as calmly as possible.

Ben sat for a moment in silence and shook his head in empathetic understanding. "I realize how strained it is for everyone right now, Pam, and I am feeling the pressure myself. Unfortunately, the company is not in a position to hire additional staff right now. The slowed economy is taking its toll on earnings, and I am being pressured to try to cut back as much as I can in every department. I am trying to do that without losing staff and without losing production. That's a real challenge, I can assure you!"

"I'm sure it is." Pam was trying to contain her frustration with the current level of stress in her department. "I just don't know what else you expect me to do."

"Well, our customers expect the deadlines to be met, and we can't bring on extra staff, so we need to find a way to increase production without additional staff. It will benefit everyone if we can."

Pam knew that increased production meant more income for everyone in her department. Bonus commissions were paid based on production, and the faster they could produce results, the more they would benefit. She also knew that everyone in the department was spread too thin as it was. She knew there were many people in her department who didn't work full-time and had to pay for day-care services. She proposed a solution.

"Ben, I have an idea that I think would work for everyone. What if we allowed some of our staff members to take some of these projects home and work on them from a 'virtual office'? Nearly everyone has computers at home with Internet access. They could access our system and complete some of the projects from home. This would allow them to commit more hours when needed without having to incur day-care expenses or the grief of spending too much time away from their families."

Ben thought for a moment and then offered his thoughts. "You know, that's not a bad idea. We could establish a set number of hours that must be fulfilled at the physical office, and then leave a flexible schedule for the virtual office. As long as the deadlines were met and production increased, there's no reason why we couldn't validate this option. Why don't you put together a formal proposal, and I will work on some ideas, too. Let's meet back in my office next Friday at the same time."

Pamela left the office with a sense of excitement and accomplishment. She knew this could be a win-win for everyone if it was put together right. She was beginning to see light at the end of the tunnel.

In all three of the scenarios above, a specific approach to resolving conflict was used. The person using the approach may not even be aware of what he is attempting to do, but the approach is still used. The three general approaches to conflict are power, rights, and reconciliation of interests.

Power—Who Is More Powerful?

This approach to resolving conflict involves the possibility of acts of aggression. Those who have the power can withhold benefits. Neither party is quite sure how far the other party will take the attack or the withdrawal.

Rights—Who Is Right and by What Standard?

This approach relies on agreed-upon rules, contracts, or minutes. Decisions are determined upon precedent, equality, and seniority.

Reconciliation of Interests

This approach takes into consideration the needs, values, and concerns of the individuals involved. It also addresses the fears and desires of both parties. This method relies on two important concepts:

◆ For every interest involved, there usually exist several possible positions that could satisfy it. A key factor is respect for everyone's participation and suggestions.

◆ Behind opposed positions lie many more compatible interests than conflicting ones. It is important to look for commonalities, interests, and solutions. The focus should be on future shared benefits for both parties.

In the first example, Patrick was using the "power approach" to resolving conflict with Jimmy. As the conflict escalated, he attempted to use aggression and force to control the conflict. Unfortunately, this is a common approach that is used in personal and professional settings. The aggression is not always physical. Sometimes it is just verbal aggression or manipulative power plays. The use of power is a very common strategy as people attempt to establish their position. The next chapter will address the use of power more specifically.

In the second example, Stan was attempting to use the "rights approach" to resolving the conflict. He was counting on the written rules and regulations of the organization to solve the problem. He referenced past notes, with which Joan could not argue. He established that a virtual contract existed and needed to be adhered to in order to alleviate conflict. This approach is often very effective in paramilitary organizations like fire departments.

In the last example, Pamela employed the "reconciliation of interests approach," which Ben bought into immediately. The stress and conflict in the organization had been mounting, and there were two sides to the conflict. Pamela and Ben were able to brainstorm a possible solution that would bring the interests of both parties together. They sought commonalities and solutions, instead of focusing only on the differences in their needs.

There are times when you may see one or more of these approaches used in a conflict scenario. You may have someone who attempts to use the rights approach. When that approach fails, he may try the power approach. You may also find a group of individuals who are using the power approach and eventually come to the reconciliation of interests approach after much discussion.

At the heart of every conflict resolution is compromise. The conflict matrix in chart 23-A depicts this concept. Look at the chart carefully.

Chart 23-A

When assertiveness and concern for self is high and concern for others and acceptance is low, force will tend to be employed in conflict. In this case, we tend to force our ideas and opinions on people, while dismissing their needs.

When assertiveness and concern for self is low and concern and acceptance for others is low, avoidance will tend to be employed in conflict. In this case, we tend to withdraw and avoid the conflict, not caring either way.

When assertiveness and concern for self is low and concern and acceptance for others is high, "your way" will tend to be employed in conflict. We accommodate other people through obligation and coexistence, but we stuff our own needs.

When assertiveness and concern for self is high and concern and acceptance for others is high, "our way" will tend to be employed in conflict. In this case, we attempt to create a win-win situation through objective problem-solving. We take into consideration the needs and interests of each other in an effort to come to the best conflict resolution possible.

At the heart of the matrix is compromise. This requires a balance of accommodating others while creating a win-win solution. We do not have to force our way, and we do not have to have someone else's way forced on us. We can bargain our positions to come to a place of compromise where everyone can win.

> Be completely humble and gentle; be patient, bearing with one another in love. Make every effort to keep the unity of the Spirit through the bond of peace (Ephesians 4:2-3).

24

Making the Confrontation

"If your brother sins, rebuke him,
and if he repents, forgive him."
—JESUS CHRIST (LUKE 17:3)

———

Jesus was pretty clear on what to do when someone sins against you. You are to go to that person and let him or her know. If the person repents, you are called to forgive and move on. Sometimes conflict deals with sin, sometimes it deals with offenses, and sometimes it deals with disagreements. In any case, approaching conflict is a very delicate process.

While confrontation is positive and healthy if done correctly, it can be detrimental if done poorly. Careful consideration should be made when confronting another person on a conflict issue. If you are an Amiable or Analytical, your tendency will be to avoid a confrontation. Try to resist this tendency and step out of your comfort zone to confront the necessary conflict in your life. If you are a Driver or an Expressive, your tendency will be to confront conflict head-on without much consideration of the process. Try to resist this tendency and think through some of the important factors below before you make the confrontation.

Pick the Right Plan

There is no perfect plan for every conflict situation you will encounter. There are, however, principles that will assist you in confrontation and conflict resolution. Your job is to seek out the most effective principles and apply them to your situation. It may require a mixing, matching, and combination of approaches. This book had been designed to give you those tools. It is important to understand social styles and how everyone is unique in approaching conflict. Methods of conflict reduction, studies of body language, and listening skills combine to make conflict resolution more productive.

Pick the Right Motivation

Before you approach someone, take the time to pray and weigh the motivation of your heart. Pray the prayer of David: "Search me, O God, and know my heart; test me and know my anxious thoughts. See if there is any offensive way in me" (Psalm 139:23-24).

Determine in your mind to take the principled approach to resolving conflict. Attempt to remain friends with anyone you face in a conflict situation. This may not be possible in every case, but it certainly should be the goal.

Determine in your mind to not strike back and get revenge. Making threats or demands will not bring resolution. It only creates more conflict. Digging in and becoming inflexible will not solve anything. It only leads to separation.

Determine in your mind to be the change agent in the conflict situation. Do not wait for the other person to make the first move. You make it. Just sitting around, waiting for the other person to change, equals no change at all. You control your part in the conflict. Face it, own it, and deal with it. Avoiding conflict and confrontation makes the situation worse. Families are disrupted, organizations suffer, and personal effectiveness is reduced. Positive confrontation is a sign of caring.

Determine in your mind to develop a thick skin. Do not take everything so personally. Relax. Ease up. Chill out a little. Do not take everything so seriously. A little humor might be what is needed. Someone once said, "We would worry less about what others think of us if we realized how seldom they do."

Determine in your mind to allow the other person to save face. Do not go for the throat. Public humiliation is not necessary. There is no reason to place a scarlet letter *C* on a person's forehead to let everyone know he is a carrier of conflict. Grow up. Be mature. Be the bigger person.

Pick the Right Time

The following principles should be kept in mind when considering the timing for a confrontation.

Poor Timing:

✦ *Rushes* the other party. It takes the person off guard. It does not give the person time to think.

✦ *Pushes* the other party to respond. It reduces the person's ability to respond in fairness, with full disclosure, and with openness.

✦ *Catches* the other party when he or she may be emotionally weak, physically tired, encountering an illness, or when the person is under time constraints.

✦ *Forces* the other party to respond negatively, especially if the confrontation takes place in a public setting where embarrassment may occur or private information is made public.

Poor timing is initiated when a person wants to catch the other party in a surprise attack. This verbal ambush can be a way to get revenge and cause hurt to someone with whom you have a disagreement. It is a selfish thing to just blurt out grievances anytime you feel like it. Wise King Solomon said, "A word aptly spoken is like apples of gold in settings of silver" (Proverbs 25:11).

It has been suggested that most family arguments occur one-half hour before dinner. This is because of poor timing. Everyone is tired from the day. Everyone is hungry. Blood-sugar levels are low and resistance is down. Individuals may have to get dinner ready or homework done, or there may be evening meetings that need to be attended. It is not a good time to start a heavy confrontation.

The second most popular time for family arguments is one-half hour before everyone leaves home for school or work. Someone may have gotten up late. The lunches need to be made, and everyone has to get dressed. All the family members are under the pressure of time deadlines. It is not a good time to start a heavy confrontation.

The same is true in a work or social setting. Outside pressures and demands on individuals have a tendency to make them edgy. If the timing is off for the person being confronted, there may be negative results.

There are occasions when married couples need to talk through some heavy issues in their relationship. When is it a good time to have this discussion? It should take place before 9:00 PM. After 9:00 PM, difficult discussions have a tendency to go downhill. This is because both of the parties are most likely tired and have many things on their agenda for the next day. Because of past experience, they know that their talk will probably not be resolved quickly. With that thought in mind, the whole discussion has a negative start.

Endeavor to have important family discussions begin before 9:00 PM. This means you may need to farm your children out to some friends or neighbors. If that cannot be done, you may need to say to your children, "Your mother and I are going to have a 'fight.'" Or you may prefer to say "a heavy discussion."

"You mean that you would actually say that to the children?" Of course. Do you really think they do not know that you argue with each other? It would probably be a healthy thing to see their parents actually work through conflict and come to a resolution. Have you ever thought about being a role model for conflict-resolution for your own family? Who is going to teach the children if you do not take the time?

If an issue cannot be resolved within an hour to an hour and a half, it might be good to table it for another time. The reason that most counseling only lasts an hour is that people tend to repeat themselves after about an hour. Take a break and approach the issue at another time with a fresh body and fresh thinking.

Good Timing:

- ✦ *The sooner the better.* As a rule, it is not good to let too much time go by between the conflict and the confrontation. First, it lets you deal with issues while they are fresh in your mind. And second, it helps to lessen the buildup of hurt or animosity that can be generated over a period of time. How long do you usually wait? What has been the pattern of how and when you face those annoying people in your life? You might consider usually dealing with the issue within four hours, with 24 hours being the longest delay. This provides you time to think through the situation and allows for unforeseen interruptions that might happen. Of course, there may be circumstances that create a need for extending the time before the confrontation. However, the concept is to do it sooner rather than later. The apostle Paul, in speaking to husbands and wives who were encountering conflict, said, "Do not let the sun go down while you are still angry" (Ephesians 4:26).

✦ *When you are feeling good.* Try and determine the best time for your schedule and the pressures you are facing. It is not good to go into a heavy discussion when you are not physically feeling good. It is better to approach the other party when you are rested and your stress level is lowered.

✦ *Set a date.* For some meetings it is good to set a specific time and date. This helps you to get organized in your thinking and prepared in your presentation. It also helps to reduce the emotional component that will be present in your discussions. By having an agreed-upon time, both parties involved will have an opportunity to think about the meeting. There will be occasions when it will not be possible to set a specific date. You may have to just wait for the right moment and opportunity to approach the individual. In this case, it is important to be prepared. You would be wise to map out or outline the items that need to be discussed. When the right moment comes, you will be ready to share your thoughts and will not be caught off guard.

✦ *Listen to your heart.* Sometimes you may not be sure when is the right time to talk with someone. In that case, get organized with what you want to share. Have it well-rehearsed in your mind. Relax. Wait patiently, and the right moment will eventually come. You will know it is the right moment when all of a sudden you find yourself alone with the person with whom you need to talk. Your heart will race a little faster, and you will ask yourself, *Is this the right time?* When you find that you cannot hold back your thoughts any longer, and you have to speak, *it will* be the right time. Learn to trust your gut. "But what if the right time doesn't come?" you ask. Then still trust your gut. When you find that you must have the issue resolved, you may need to take the initiative. Go ahead. Remember, you have prepared for this meeting.

Pick the Right Place

The ideal location for confrontation is neutral territory. Remember, in most sports activities the home team has the advantage. The same is true in heavy or difficult discussions. Whoever's turf that the confrontation takes place on has a slight advantage. Neutral ground could be at a local restaurant. Talking over issues in public often keeps emotions from rising to an unproductive level. Neutral ground could be on a park bench or on a walk. Discussing issues while on a walk is very effective. The walking itself lets off a lot of nervous energy that may be present. It does not require continued eye contact that is sometimes difficult to maintain. It also helps both parties focus on the decision as they are moving forward. It is almost like they are discussing a third-party issue that is in front of them. Many husbands and wives find that this is a positive and productive way to talk over many of their disagreements.

Of course, some issues cannot be discussed in public. They must be dealt with strictly on a private level. Some matters need eye-to-eye contact. And, in a less-than-perfect world, we are not always able to choose neutral territory. In these cases, go ahead and make the best of the conversation, regardless of where you happen to be.

What do you do if you are caught in a situation where it is the wrong time and the wrong place? Take a deep breath. Determine to be mature and controlled. Attempt to assess what the real issue is. Listen carefully to what is being said and to the emotion behind it. Try not to take it too personally and lose perspective. And rise to the occasion with the proper response.

A number of years ago, I was in a hotel lobby with a group of friends. One of the individuals in the group was not happy with what the group wanted to do. He had made plans for the day for the entire group without asking them. When he shared his previously planned schedule with the group, they were not excited about it. They wanted to take the day's activities in another direction.

At this point, the individual began to throw an adult temper tantrum in the hotel lobby. He raised his voice and made accusations. He put people down. He was very vocal and created a scene that drew the attention of everyone in the hotel. We were all embarrassed and caught off guard. He made his final closing statement and was about to stomp off.

With increased volume in my voice, I said, "Oh no, you don't! You don't create a public scene and just walk off. We are going to stay right here and finish this discussion." Everyone in the group turned and looked at me. You can well believe that everyone in the lobby was also really interested now. The stage was definitely set for a confrontation.

If this particular conflict would have been allowed to occur in public and had not been addressed when it happened, it would have taught that individual that he could say anything and then just retreat. He would continue to use his manipulative hit-and-run behavior as a scare tactic. The mature and adult thing was to confront behavior that was unacceptable.

In most situations, I prefer to talk with people in a private setting. However, we do not always have that luxury. You can mark it down as a general rule: If someone makes an issue public, you have to deal with the issue publicly.

Pick the Right Goal

In any attempt to resolve conflict, it is important to pick the right goal. How would you like to see the discussion end? What outcome would be best for all parties involved? What would be the ideal solution?

It is important to enter the confrontation with a positive outcome in mind. Your attitude will play a significant part in the entire encounter. If you enter the confrontation with the desire to hurt the other party, you will probably succeed. If you desire to get revenge, you most likely will. If you want to let the other party know you are mad, you may encounter a self-fulfilled wish.

You can enter the confrontation with the desire to see change. You can be positive, even if the other person is negative. You can help set the tone for mutual resolution. Remember, you *will* reap what you sow.

What changes would you like to see occur in the situation or between people? Someone has said, "If you aim at nothing, you will hit it every time." A fuzzy goal or objective will end in a fuzzy resolution.

In helping to determine your goals, you need to understand that everything may not work out the way you desire. You may have to make some adjustments in your own thinking. You may need to develop alternatives and backup plans.

You might consider making three lists. The first list would include the ideal results you would like to see. The second list could focus on the things you may not totally like but would accept. This would include things you would be willing to give up and things that you would change for the other party. The third list would be your bottom line. What things would you not give up? What things would you fight for? What things would put your back against the wall?

Once you have established some guidelines for your confrontation, you can take steps to resolve the conflict. The next factor you must consider is the words you will use when you initiate the confrontation. Chapter 25 will provide you with some practical tools for choosing your words carefully.

> A fool's lips bring him strife, and his mouth invites a beating (Proverbs 18:6).

Hopefully, this next chapter will help you avoid the label of a fool and the strife and potential verbal beating that comes with the use of unwise words!

25

Choose Your Words Carefully

When words are many, sin is not absent,
but he who holds his tongue is wise.
—Proverbs 10:19

———

Choosing your words carefully is one of the keys to successful conflict resolution. The words you choose can create defensiveness or acceptance. Your words can cause someone to dismiss your message or accept it. This section will provide some valuable tools in approaching conflict.

One of the keys to effective conflict resolution is to use "I" statements rather than "you" statements. "I" statements are assertive and confrontive. "You" statements are aggressive and attacking. "I" statements let the other party know that you have strong ideas and convictions. It gives the person a gauge of how strongly you feel about a certain issue. Your strong beliefs and emotions can be shared without attacking the other person. You are simply letting the other person know how you think and feel about the conflict between you. If you respond by saying, "You idiot," the war will probably be on.

The wonderful thing about "I" statements is that you can talk about both positive or negative thoughts and feelings. The use of "I" statements reduces the risk of the separation of parties. You do not have to start the conversation on a strong level. You can slowly and gently raise or lower the intensity as needed.

+ "When you embarrassed me in the meeting, I felt *surprised* and caught off guard."

+ "When you embarrassed me in the meeting, I felt a little *annoyed*."

+ "When you embarrassed me in the meeting, I felt *irritated*."

+ "When you embarrassed me in the meeting, I felt hurt and *disgusted*."

+ "When you embarrassed me in the meeting, I felt very *angry*."

"I" statements help you focus on behavior and reduce the probability of attacking the other party on a personal basis. The use of "I" statements helps you to crystallize your thinking and organize your presentation of the issue. This clarity of thinking will help keep you on track so you do not stray from the central conflict.

Another wonderful benefit from the use of "I" statements is that they help to bleed off the tension you are feeling. This is especially important if and when the other party does not admit to any part in the conflict or will not change his or her behavior.

The power of "I" statements gives clarity, focuses thinking, and reduces personal and group tension. The result is that these statements often create more confidence in the individual initiating the confrontation. "I" statements also create a platform for true communication to take place. They can also help to increase respect in the confronted party because the confronter is being personally honest and straightforward. This type of communication can help to strengthen relationships and bonds between people.

I have a friend who had to confront his next-door neighbor over a very emotionally loaded situation. His daughter came to him one day and related how the next-door neighbor had been touching her (over her clothes) in the private areas of her body. She was about seven at the time.

Understandably, my friend was very angry and protective. He shared with me the struggle he went through. He was, naturally, full of strong emotions. He was a father, a counselor, and a man. He was trained in the martial arts and knew how to kill in self-defense. He had been trained in conflict resolution, yet it was hard to control all of his emotions over this most personal issue.

When he went next door to confront the matter, he knew he had to be in control of his thoughts and emotions. When the neighbor opened the door, my friend said, "I'm so mad at you, I could rip you to pieces!"

He went on to relate to me that

> I had to use "I" statements. Even if I was extremely mad, I had to let him know how I was feeling and how important the issue was to me. If I would have used "you" statements and attacked him personally, he might have responded with his own "you" words. That would have most likely escalated the situation to an out-of-control level. At that point, the headlines the following day about me may have read, "Enraged Father Kills Next Door Neighbor."

Using "I" statements will help you, even in the most difficult situations.

A second key concept is to attack or deal with the issue and not the person. This requires sticking to facts and actual behavior. It

> *Effective confrontation is telling another person the effect that his or her behavior has on you.*

is important not to try and second-guess the motivation behind the behavior. When you deal with just the behavior at hand and not the motivation, it opens the door for change. All people tend to resent it and get angry when their motivation is under attack. Even if you are correct in your evaluation, the pride of other people and the desire to save face will keep them from responding in a positive manner.

A third key is to attempt to stay away from time-bomb words—those phrases that tend to blow the situation out of proportion. "You *always* forget to call home when you're going to be late." "*Every time* we get into a discussion you get mad." "You *never* do anything right." "You're *forever* complaining." "You *constantly* interrupt me when I'm talking." "*Every moment* we're together seems to be filled with arguments." "Can't you do *anything* right?" "Trying to talk to you is a *never-ending* struggle."

The above types of cataclysmic statements only broaden and escalate conflict. They blow up in the other person's mind and hinder progress. They sidetrack the real issues. People who are being attacked by absolutes defend themselves by responding to the hostility focused in their direction. Or they turn around and attack the other person in retaliation. "I remember that I called you last Tuesday night and told you I would be late." "I wasn't mad when we talked about this at breakfast." "I cleaned up the garage like you asked me to." "I don't complain half as much as you do." "Talk about being interrupted. I can't even get a word in edgewise." "We weren't arguing when we went to dinner with Ted and Sally." "You're right, I can't do anything right. I couldn't even marry the right person." "Well, if it is so much of a struggle, maybe we had better part ways."

The fourth key is to learn to be specific rather than general in your comments. If there is a conflict between you and someone else, you

> **The goal of confrontation is to get your own needs met without the other person becoming and remaining defensive.**

will need to share with that person the concrete and tangible effect they are having in your life. The purpose of this is to get the person to change his or her behavior.

A change in a person's behaviors and attitudes does not always take place when confrontation occurs. Sometimes it will take weeks or months. Confrontation is simply a defense of one's own rights in a nonjudgmental manner. Hopefully, resolution will take place on the sooner side rather than on the longer side.

Below is a suggested four-part confrontation message. It is designed to assist you in forming your thoughts about conflict situations. It will help you to stay on track in your meeting with the annoying individuals in your life. It is a matrix that can be applied at home, at work, or in the community.

Four-Part Confrontation Message			
When You	**I Feel**	**Because**	**I Would Like**
In a non-judgmental manner, describe the conflicting or offending behavior in specific and concrete terms.	In a non-judgmental manner, disclose your feelings about the conflicting or offending behavior.	In a non-judgmental manner, state the concrete and tangible effect on you and your schedule.	In a non-judgmental manner, state the specific and tangible behavior that you would like to see changed.

When You—In the process of describing the undesired behavior, be sure to be accurate and specific. The description of the behavior should be kept as brief as possible. It should go right to the point in crystal-clear terms. Be careful not to use time-bomb words or absolutes like *always, never,* and *every time.*

I Feel—The disclosure of feelings should accurately reflect the intensity of your emotion. If you are angry, own your anger with "I" words. If you are only a little irritated, do not exaggerate and make it sound worse than it is. Clearly state your irritation. Try not to use words that make judgment statements or are designed to hurt the individual being confronted. An example of a judgment word would be *disappointed.* That word is often used to make the other person feel guilty.

Because—In the process of sharing the tangible effect of the offending behavior, try not to turn it into a relationship problem. Keep the description of the effect objective rather than subjective. To help make the issue concrete, you may need to share how the behavior has cost you money. The actions of the offending party may have harmed your possessions. Those actions may have cost you extra time or interfered with your work effectiveness. The person's conduct may endanger your job or reputation.

I Would Like—The resolution of conflict is usually oriented toward the future. For this reason, it is important to clearly state the behavior that you believe is acceptable. This gives a goal to work toward and an opportunity to change. Along with what you would like to see changed, it is good to share what you are willing to do to help the resolution be successful. When both parties work toward a shared goal, it engenders hope to all parties. It helps to bring about resolution and harmony.

In considering the delivery of your four-part message, it is good to ask yourself, "Do I have a right to confront?" This helps you filter out your motivation and determine your possible approach. There are different approaches when we talk to a boss, a fellow worker, a friend, or a family member.

It might be good for you to write out your message. This will help you to be specific and not wander. You also might be wise to ask yourself, "Is it worth it? Could this be risky for a relationship or a job?"

Sometimes confrontation is necessary and must be done. At other times, it is good to have thick skin and simply let things run off our backs. King Solomon said, "A man's wisdom gives him patience; it is to his glory to overlook an offense" (Proverbs 19:11).

You might find it helpful to role-play with a friend who could pretend to be the individual to be confronted. This practice will help keep you from becoming confused or stumbling over your words. Your friend could give you helpful hints, and maybe even suggest that you better not say a particular thought. If you do not feel comfortable sharing with a friend, you would do well to rehearse anyway, even in private.

Once you decide that a confrontation must take place, do not put it off for a long period of time. This will only make it worse. Be sure to be consistent in your message. It must make sense and should not add a host of unnecessary details. These details often confuse the issue and sidetrack both parties from the heart of the matter.

You can expect the other person to become defensive. After your first presentation of the four-part "When You / I Feel / Because / I Would Like" message, stop and let the person respond. You will need to actively listen to what he or she is saying. There may be some tension. Do not run from it. When the tension lowers, return to your original message.

Even though confrontation may take place, it does not mean that resolution has occurred. Resolution begins to take place when the other party buys into and owns his or her half of the problem. It must be followed by a mutually agreed-upon solution to solve the difficulty. There should also be follow-up to ensure the effectiveness of the solution.

Unfortunately, not all confrontation with annoying people is successful. When a confrontation has fallen on deaf ears, it might be time to go back to the drawing board. You might ask yourself, "Was I too judgmental? Was I not specific enough about the tangible effect on me? Did I send an inconsistent message? Did I pussyfoot around and sugarcoat the message and let the person off the responsibility hook?" Or worse, "Did I get angry and say some things I should not have? Did I contribute to making the problem worse by arguing?"

One of the most common responses to confrontation is defensiveness. Sometimes defensiveness is more passive in nature than overt. Body language is often a good indicator of the level of defensiveness or acceptance when it comes to conflict resolution. The next section will provide you with some guidelines for identifying and dealing with different types of body language.

26

Observing Body Language

He alone is an acute observer, who can observe
minutely without being observed.
—Johann Kaspar Lavater

Have you ever just sat and watched the behavior of people in a public place? It can be quite educational and sometimes very amusing. To help you learn to observe behavior more objectively, I suggest that the next time you are in a public place (a shopping mall, airport, or doctor's office) that you observe:

✦ How people walk…fast or slow

✦ How people talk…loudly or quietly

✦ People's facial expressions…animated or controlled

✦ The tone of voice…happy or sad, high-pitched or low-pitched

✦ An individual's posture…rigid or relaxed

✦ Eye contact…direct or indirect

✦ Speech content…facts or feelings

✦ Body gestures…many or few

✦ Reaction to other people…outgoing or restrained

✦ Response under stress…angry or fearful

We all tend to listen to other people and watch their behavior half-heartedly. We then quickly move from casual observation to subjective evaluation and judgment. Many times our hasty judgments result in emotional turmoil, producing annoying relationships and conflict between people.

The poet Robert Burns extolled the virtue of seeing ourselves as other people see us. How do your loved ones see you? Can they predict your behavior? We like to think of our own behavior as less predictable than that of other people. We often think of ourselves as more complex and more difficult to understand. Many times we look in the mirror and see only what we want to see. Francis Quarles wrote, "If thou seest anything in thyself which may make thee proud, look a little further and thou shall find enough to humble thee; if thou be wise, view the peacock's feathers with his feet. And weigh thy best parts with thy imperfections."

The more we become aware of the behavior of other people and ourselves, the more we will be able to control our responses. And learning to control our responses and reactions in our relationships will reduce tensions and help us get along better. King Solomon said, "A gentle answer turns away wrath, but a harsh word stirs up anger" (Proverbs 15:1). Our behavior and our reactions to the behavior of other people can positively influence our relationships.

The study of body language or body signals is called *kinesics*. Kinesics involves any form of body movement, including those brought about by conscious thought and those movements that are reflexive or involuntary. When we wave good-bye to someone, it is a voluntary action consciously chosen by our brain.

We do, however, have many body movements or signals that are not consciously chosen. Studies have been done on the pupils of men's eyes while viewing various photographs. When a photograph of a nude woman comes on the screen, the pupils of men's eyes automatically and involuntarily widen or enlarge. The men in the testing did not consciously say, "I am now going to widen my pupils while I look at this picture." It just happened. They could not control that particular reaction.

In learning to communicate effectively and get along with both the friendly people and the annoying people in our lives, it is important to understand body language. The various body signals of other people can give you clues to what others are thinking and how they are feeling.

Understanding body language can help you reduce conflict and break through defenses of your family, friends, and working associates. Learning to read body signals will enhance your ability to be alert to the needs of everyone with whom you come in contact.

For many years people have discussed the merits of "women's intuition." Some women seem to possess an uncanny ability to understand the feelings and motivations of other people. Where does this unique ability come from? How are these women able to know, without the use of a rational thinking process? In the field of law enforcement, some police officers have the unique ability to sense when an individual is about to commit a crime. They seem to know that something is wrong or something bad is about to happen. They call this intuitive knowledge the "hink." They might say, "I've got a hinky feeling that that guy is about to sell some drugs." How do they sense this precriminal behavior?

In both of the above cases, neither the women nor the police officers have any special magical powers. What they are sensing, feeling, or knowing about people comes from their ability to accurately read the nonverbal behavior of the people they are observing. As a general rule, women are usually more perceptive in reading body signals than men.

This book was not written to be the definitive last word on body language. We have only limited space to discuss this important issue. However, it is hoped that this introduction will stir your interest and cause you to pursue further education on this topic.

As you attempt to become more skilled in reading nonverbal behavior, remember to look for clusters of body signals. They are communicating a message. An individual body gesture could be compared to a single word in a sentence. A grouping of body gestures (a cluster) can be compared to the entire sentence.

In other words, it is important to look for consistency, unity, and congruence. It is possible to misread body signals if each individual signal is separated from other signals. For example, let's take the body signal of folding the arms across the chest while talking or listening to someone. This gesture, by itself, is generally considered a barrier or a hostile gesture. But what if there were other incongruent body signals accompanying the folded arms? What if the person was laughing and joking at the same time as having the folded arms? That would be a mixed message. You would have to keep watching to see if other signals would clarify the reason for the folded arms.

The person might have his arms folded because he is cold. He might be folding his arms because someone else in the group has his arms folded. He might have a sore back, and folding his arms supports the back muscles. Perhaps his arms were folded because he was telling a story about someone with folded arms. Now if the arms are folded, the legs are crossed, there is a frown on his face, and he is gritting his teeth, then you probably have a hostile person. The cluster of gestures is consistent.

In the study of body language, it is also important to understand territorial space or zones. Chart 26-A displays the different zones and the amount of space people normally expect in each of the zones.

	Intimate Space Zone	Personal Space Zone	Social Space Zone	Public Space Zone
	6 to 18 inches	18 Inches to 4 Feet	4 to 12 Feet	Over 12 Feet

Chart 26-A

Everyone has an *intimate zone* where only special people can enter. This might include those who are emotionally close, like a spouse, children, friends, relatives, or someone the person is dating. The *personal zone* is expanded to include fellow office workers, people at parties or social functions, and salespeople.

The *social zone* is where we usually keep strangers or people whom we have just recently met. We often stand farther away from the gardener doing yard work and the repairman fixing our air-conditioning. In this area we are polite and friendly, but a little distant and reserved at the same time.

The *public zone* is the area in which a lot of strangers are put together as a group. This could include people at concerts, theaters, ball games, parks, amusement centers, or the shopping mall. At these events or places, everyone is physically at the same place, while being emotionally in his or her own world.

These four zones may not always be consciously on our mind. However, if someone enters these zones uninvited, we begin to feel nervous, irritated, angry, and will sometimes even physically strike back. Law enforcement agencies understand territorial space very well. They know that if people are crowded together they become hostile—the greater the density of the group, the greater the anger of the mob. Because of this, the police will endeavor to break up the group. As the crowd disperses, the individual people regain their personal space. When personal space is reestablished, people calm down.

On the reverse side, law enforcement agencies will sometimes purposely enter a suspect's personal or intimate space. They know that this makes the person nervous and angry. In his nervousness and anxiety, the suspect will often respond with more information or will not be able to maintain a consistent story line. This invasion of a person's space helps to break down defenses.

If you have an annoying person in your life, just try and enter his or her personal or intimate territory without being invited. Your difficulties will immediately increase.

We have all experienced the unwritten territorial rules in our crowded society. When riding an elevator, almost everyone watches the numbers above the door rather than looking around. Seldom do we talk to strangers on the bus or on the subway. We avoid eye contact with others as much as possible. We try not to stare when someone has a physical defect or when people have tattoos all over their bodies.

At the theater, we put our coats on seats we are reserving for other people. We put our books on the table at the library in front of the chair we want. We save spaces in lines for our friends. Research indicates that 90 percent of the time, people choose the end toilets in public restrooms. Who created all of these unwritten rules? Where did the rules come from? How are they maintained?

Basically, the whole system has been created and passed on through the use of nonverbal body language.

Interesting Facts About Body Language

✦ In over 2000 videotaped conflict negotiations, never once was a conflict settled where anyone in attendance had crossed legs. Settlement was reached only when negotiators uncrossed their legs and moved toward each other (Gerald Nierenberg and Henry Calero).

✦ Mothers whose voices registered high on anxiety had daughters who were more attentive and cautious.

✦ Studies have shown that when a teacher's voice rises in tone and the words are rapid, the classroom disruption goes up proportionately. As the teacher lowers his or her tone, speaks more slowly, and uses words carefully, negative classroom behavior decreases. My father taught me that long ago. He said, "If…you do that…one…more…time… you are in. . .trouble." End of story.

✦ Studies of mothers with emotionally disturbed children show that they send more conflicting verbal and nonverbal messages than mothers of normal children.

✦ People who live in the city shake hands with their elbows bent. They stand about 18 inches apart. People who live in the country lean forward and shake hands with their arms fully extended, their elbows locked, and at a farther distance apart.

✦ Wives are extremely alert to other women entering their husband's personal or intimate territory. Even if the husband is not aware of the invasion, the wife is.

✦ Studies indicate that a library table can be reserved by simply placing books on the table in front of the chair. This act can reserve the table up to 70 minutes. If someone leaves a coat on the chair, this action can reserve the table up to two hours.

✦ An individual's status can be determined by the amount of time he takes to enter a room or to answer a door. The faster a person enters the room, and the slower he answers the door, the more status he has. Employees usually do not enter their boss's office unless invited.

✦ One of the most irritating body gestures is to point a finger at someone. The second is to give them the "finger."

✦ Individuals who are tall seem to be more successful in relationships as they decrease their height when dealing with people. They sit down in a chair or on a desk or lower themselves a little when talking to other people. This helps to decrease the dominance naturally afforded to them by their height alone.

✦ Successful people seem to initiate handshaking more than unsuccessful people.

✦ People who are more introverted seem to keep people at a greater conversational distance than extroverts.

✦ People who grab their hands behind their back are showing signs of restraint. When they grab higher on their arm, they are probably angry.

✦ When people are attempting to make guarded statements or deceive, they will often put their hand to their mouth and make a fake coughing gesture.

- When people start yawning, they usually continue to yawn from 14-17 times before they stop.

- When people put their fingers or other objects in their mouth, it could indicate that they are feeling under pressure.

- The drumming of fingers on a table is often viewed as boredom. More likely it is a sign of impatience.

- A study was done on two groups of students listening to a lecture. The first group was instructed to listen with their arms crossed. The second group was to listen with their arms uncrossed. The crossed-arm group retained and learned 38 percent less than the uncrossed-arm group.

> *Trust not a man's words if you please, or you may come to very erroneous conclusions; but at all times place implicit confidence in a man's countenance in which there is no deceit and of necessity there can be none.*
>
> —GEORGE BORROW

- People who are nervous will grasp onto something and hold it in front of them. If they have nothing to hold, they may grasp their own wrist or fiddle with their watch.

- On job interviews, applicants who have their ankles locked during the interview may be holding back something.

- When a person is excited, his pupils will dilate up to four times his normal size. If the person is angry, his pupils will contract.

- Smokers who feel confident will blow their smoke upward. Those who feel negative or more depressed will blow their smoke downward.

◆ The more a person who smokes plays with or moves his cigarette, cigar, or pipe, the more nervous he is. When he stops smoking, he is probably more relaxed.

◆ When people begin to mirror the nonverbal behavior of the other person, it is usually a compliment or a way of saying, "I agree with you," or "I like you."

◆ When two people are talking and a third party walks over, if they point one of their toes toward the person, it indicates that the person is accepted into the group. If not, the third party will get the message and leave.

◆ People who sit with their back against a wall or partition show lesser heart rate and blood pressure than those whose backs face a doorway, window, or an open room.

◆ When walking toward someone, there will be a meeting of the eyes. Next there will be a very slight eye click by one or both of the parties. The eyes will either click to the right or the left. This tells the one person which way the other person is going to walk. When you bump into someone, it is only because you did not pick up on the eye click.

◆ When caught looking at someone, the unwritten rule is to look away. If a woman does not look away from a man, she is giving him an invitation to approach. If the man continues to look, it means that he is interested.

> *He that has eyes to see and ears to hear may convince himself that no mortal can keep a secret. If his lips are silent, he chatters with his fingertips; betrayal oozes out of him at every pore.*
>
> —SIGMUND FREUD

◆ When people get caught in a lie, it is usually because of one of three reasons: 1) They want to be caught; 2) They feel guilty; 3) They do not know how to monitor their own nonverbal body language.

Learning to observe and understand body language will assist you in conflict prevention and resolution. As you are communicating with other people, you will begin to pick up defensive or offensive signals. This gives you the opportunity to stop and ask questions or redirect your method of communication. Try to use the observation of body language to improve the personal and professional relationships in your life.

> *Look in the face of the person to whom you are speaking if you wish to know his real sentiments, for he can command his words more easily than his countenance.*
>
> —LORD CHESTERFIELD

27

Listening to Reduce Conflict

Everyone should be quick to listen,
slow to speak, and slow to become angry.
—James 1:19

———

"Kurt, can I talk to you for a minute?" Amber cornered him just as he was walking out of the conference room. She was a little perturbed with him after he had dismissed one of her ideas in the recent company brainstorming meeting.

"Uh, okay...I guess so. What's up, Amber?" Kurt was in a hurry and did not particularly want to deal with Amber right then. They had been experiencing some tension between them. Amber seemed to spread negativity throughout the organization, and Kurt would rather avoid her.

"Can we go into your office, Kurt? I have something I want to discuss with you."

"Sure." Kurt sighed heavily and led the way. Amber followed him into his office, and they both sat down. Kurt began thumbing through his messages while Amber mustered up the nerve to say what was on her mind. She started wringing her hands as she began to talk.

"I just wanted to tell you how frustrated I was in that last meeting. As soon as I started to share my idea, you just cut me off and dismissed my input like it didn't matter. It just seems like—"

"I wasn't trying to demean your input, Amber." Kurt cut her off before she could finish her sentence. "I already knew how you felt about my proposal, and I didn't want you to spread your negativism."

"What is that supposed to mean?" Amber crossed her arms over her chest.

"It just means that you are very negative, and I knew if you started in, you would turn other people against my idea. I just didn't want—" Amber cut him off before he could finish.

"Just stop right there, Kurt. That's a crock and you know it. Just because I want people to look at all sides of the issue does not make me negative. You just think everyone should see it your way or—" Kurt jumped in and started talking again.

"You're doing it right now! You just look at the negative side of everything, and it's annoying!" Kurt was getting upset.

"Well, you just cut me off for the third time today, which you do constantly. I can't talk to you!" Amber stood up and stormed out of the room.

"Good riddance," Kurt mumbled under his breath as he walked over and slammed the door behind her.

Unfortunately, this type of exchange is very common. When people attempt to resolve conflict, they often hold strongly to their own position. When they feel like that position is being violated or invalidated, they will defend it even stronger. One of the fastest

> *A fool finds no pleasure in understanding but delights in airing his own opinions.*
>
> —PROVERBS 18:2

ways to invalidate someone's position, ideas, or views is to refuse to listen.

Cutting people off or interrupting them while they are talking is a common practice that merely escalates conflict. People will raise their voice to be heard or completely withdraw in rebellion at the invalidation. Sometimes we have to stop and ask ourselves, "Is the goal here to prove I am right, or is it to resolve a conflict and have all parties feel validated in their position?"

If you are standing across the room and say something to someone and the person cannot hear you, what do you do? Normally, you talk louder. If someone is across the street and cannot hear you, you shout until they can hear. Well, that is also how people respond in conflict. If they bring up an issue and they feel they are not being heard, they will merely talk louder. If they still feel they are not being heard, they will shout. Sometimes the shouting is passive in nature and consists of a complete withdrawal from the situation. Sometimes the shouting is literal, as voices are raised and tempers flare.

One of the keys to reducing conflict is to hear and be heard. How is that done? Very carefully! Active listening takes a tremendous amount of energy and patience. When used properly, it will build bridges and reduce conflicts. When people feel heard, they do not feel a need to demand recognition of their point or position. They received that recognition in the listening process. Do you consider yourself a good listener?

> An old man goes to his doctor and says, "I don't think my wife's hearing is as good as it used to be. What should I do?"
>
> The doctor replies, "Try this test to find out for sure. When your wife is in the kitchen doing dishes, stand 15 feet behind her and ask her a question. If she

doesn't respond, move about five feet closer and try again. If she still doesn't respond, keep moving closer, asking the question until she hears you."

The man goes home and sees his wife preparing dinner. He stands 15 feet behind her and says, "What's for dinner, honey?" No response. He moves to ten feet behind her and asks again, no response. He moves within five feet, and asks, "Honey, what's for dinner?" Still no answer.

Finally he stands directly behind her and says, "Honey, what's for dinner?"

She spins around toward him and shouts, "For the fourth time, *I said 'chicken!'*"

Most people think they are great listeners and it is everyone else who has the problem. While many people feel they listen well, few really do. Listening is not merely sitting quietly and allowing someone to rant and rave about feelings or an issue. Listening is not tapping your foot while you anxiously wait for the person to finish a sentence. Listening is not thinking about your response or comeback while the other person is spilling his guts. Listening is not thinking about what you have to do tomorrow while someone is talking to you. Listening is not remaining silent while someone talks as you divide your attention between the papers on your desk and the person speaking. Active listening takes work.

What Is Active Listening?

Active listening is not an easy task. It takes commitment, especially if you are dealing with one of the annoying people in your life. Listening is hard enough when everything is going smoothly, but even more difficult when conflict is involved. Not only does it take energy to listen carefully, but it also takes energy to not become defensive yourself. It takes energy to control your own temper and be calm. It takes energy to not jump to conclusions. Listening requires patience.

Attentive listening is an act of kindness. It is an act of caring, and it takes concentration. It takes effort to turn the focus from your own thoughts and emotions to those of the one to whom you are listening. It requires our attempt to listen as if we were in the other person's shoes and walking his or her path. It is a compliment to the other person when we listen.

Active listening is not just receiving the intended message, but making the other person feel heard. The first step in active listening is giving our undivided attention to the person who is speaking. This means that we are not multitasking while the person is talking to us. The best communication is in person, but sometimes issues need to be dealt with over the phone. When someone is talking over the phone about an issue, it is easy to get sidetracked and begin doing other things because we do not have to make eye contact. We need to resist this urge and give our full attention so we can completely absorb the true message.

If we are communicating with someone in person, it is important that we give that person our undivided attention. As a listener, we must become conscious of our own behaviors that may distract from the listening process. We may have the habit of fiddling with pencils or keys. We may jingle change in our pocket, fidget nervously, or drum our fingers. These behaviors do not help us in the listening process. When we are cracking our knuckles, frequently shifting weight, or crossing and uncrossing our legs, it causes distractions. Swinging a crossed leg up and down, watching a TV program across the room, or waving and nodding to other people sends a negative message to the speaker. It says, "I'm not interested."

To be an effective listener, we often have to sacrifice our time. We have to decline to take phone calls. We have to stop typing on the computer while people are talking to us. Our own workload may increase as we exercise the difficult task of active listening.

Eye contact is also very important. We need to focus on the speaker and what he or she is saying, rather than looking around the room. Have you ever spoken to someone only to find that person looking past you? You cannot tell if he is bored, wants to talk to someone else, or is simply not interested. When you make consistent eye contact with the person who is talking to you, the message is being sent that you are listening.

> *Loan a man your ears and you will immediately open a pathway to his heart.*

When you make eye contact, it should be on the same level as the person talking. If you stand up and look down on the person, you may project a negative sense of domination or power. If you are sitting and the other person is standing, you may experience the same effect in reverse. Level eye contact lends itself to a more cohesive listening environment and keeps everyone on the same level.

Now that you have provided your undivided attention and are maintaining eye contact, *listen*. This means your mouth and your mind are both quiet while you actually process what the person is trying to say. Your mind cannot properly assess the intended message if it is busy racing about with other thoughts.

As the person begins to relay his underlying feelings and/or message, emotions may rise or frustration may emerge. The person may also make absolute statements like, "You always…" or "You never…" The person may exaggerate the situation or describe it differently than you see it. This would be a very tempting time for you to cut the person off and set him straight. This would also be a very tempting time to correct the areas where the person is blatantly wrong. As hard as it may be, resist this temptation and listen to the *entire* message.

For most people, this is probably the most difficult stage in the listening process. A nagging urge to jump in usually overcomes the listener who just cannot help but interrupt. As a result, the person talking feels invalidated and becomes more adamant about expressing his or her views. Even in casual conversation, interrupting is rude. It sends a message to the other person that what you have to say is much more important than what the other person was saying. It sends a message that you do not value the thoughts of the other person.

People often use excuses for interrupting. "I'm just trying to add to the conversation." "I was just interjecting." "If I didn't say something, I would have forgotten." "Well, you talk too long, and I have things to say, too." "Well, you cut me off, too!" There's really no good excuse for interrupting people or finishing their sentences for them. If you want to send a message that you value the opinion of other people and you want to make them feel heard, you really have to listen. Having said that, if you are the talker, do not abuse someone's willingness to listen to you! Take little breaks and allow the other person to share thoughts and feelings as well.

Now that you have given your undivided attention, you are making eye contact, and you are listening and not interrupting, you can begin to "reflect back." This is an important step in the active listening process.

What Is "Reflecting Back"?

After you have given someone the opportunity to really speak his or her mind, allow yourself a moment to absorb all that was said. Instead of telling your side of the issue, take the time to let the person know he or she was heard. This takes a little more than saying, "Okay, I have heard you, so now hear me." Letting someone know he or she has been heard takes a process of reflecting back. When you reflect back to someone, you are expressing back to them what you heard and making sure the intended message was what you received. It also gives the other party an opportunity to offer clarification, if needed, before you state your position. Someone is much more likely to be receptive to your views and positions once that person feels he or she has been heard and understood.

Let's go back to the conversation with Amber and Kurt and look at an example of what reflecting back looks like. Amber started out with, "I just wanted to tell you how frustrated I was in that last meeting. As soon as I started to share my idea, you just cut me off and dismissed my input like it didn't matter. It just seems like—"

At that point, Kurt cut her off, which frustrated Amber even more. She then proceeded to cut him off, and the conflict escalated. Had Kurt let her get it all off her chest and then reflected back, the conversation may have evolved like this:

> *Amber:* "I just wanted to tell you how frustrated I was in that last meeting. As soon as I started to share my idea, you just cut me off and dismissed my input like it didn't matter. It just seems like you don't care what I think. I had some really good ideas I wanted to add, and you just passed over me. That really hurt my feelings, Kurt."
>
> *Kurt* (after a short pause): "So if I understand you correctly, you feel like I wasn't listening to your ideas and just cut you off. That made you feel like your

opinion didn't matter, and I hurt your feelings. It sounds like you are a little annoyed with me. Is that correct?"

Amber: "Yes, that's exactly what I was feeling. I'm sure you weren't trying to be mean, but it seems like you haven't been open to my input lately."

Kurt: "So you also feel like I have been negating your input in some other areas as well, and you feel frustrated with me. Is that right?"

Amber: "Yes, that's how I have been feeling."

At this point, Kurt has not agreed with Amber and told her that she was correct and he was wrong. He has not defended his position or become defensive. He has simply made her feel heard and let her know that her intended message was received and he was listening. Now that she has felt heard, she is more apt to listen to Kurt's feelings and opinions.

Kurt: "I can understand why you might be feeling that way. I did cut you off and dismiss your input in the meeting. I didn't mean to be rude, it's just that I knew you were already against my proposal, and I felt like you would turn everyone else against it. I have been avoiding your input in other areas somewhat, because I felt you might shoot them down. It just seems like you approach some of the ideas around here with a very critical eye."

Amber: "It sounds like you've been feeling frustrated with me as well. I hear you saying that you feel like I would have turned everyone against your idea in the meeting, and that's why you didn't let me finish my input. Is that right?"

Kurt: "Yes, that's right."

Amber: "And you also feel like I have been pretty negative about ideas lately?"

Kurt: "Yes. I believe that you just want to be sure everything gets done right, but sometimes it comes across as negative."

Amber: "I can see where it might come across that way. I will try harder to present my input in a more positive way, and I would appreciate it if you would hear me all the way out. I think we both have a lot to offer in these brainstorming sessions, so let's try to respect each other's opinions a little more."

Kurt: "I think that's fair. Thanks for coming and sharing your concerns with me." Then they both stood up and hugged. (Okay, maybe that is taking it too far, but one of them did not go stomping out of the office in a rage. Active listening really does work.)

After each person had thoroughly listened to the other and then reflected back, both were able to gain a sense of validation and understanding. If we want other people to hear and understand us, we have to be willing to first hear them and understand their position. When we do this, walls come down, defenses drop, and bridges are built.

Reflective statements might include:

- ✦ "As I get it…"
- ✦ "In other words…"
- ✦ "I hear you saying…"
- ✦ "So what you're saying is…"
- ✦ "You want to…"

✦ "You believe..."

✦ "I'm sensing that..."

✦ "You're feeling that..."

✦ "You think we should..."

Reflective statements might include clarification questions:

✦ "Am I safe to assume that you mean...?"

✦ "I hear you saying...but I'm not sure what you mean. Will you explain this further?"

✦ "I'm totally confused. Would you explain more?"

✦ "I think I hear you saying...Do I understand you correctly?"

✦ "Would you please tell me more about ...?"

✦ "Help me out. I am not sure I understand what you are saying."

✦ "Let me share with you my impression, and you help me to see if we are on the same page."

Clarification statements or questions should be expressed in a tentative manner. In this way, the speaker can clear up any misunderstanding. It lets people know that you are not being judgmental but are listening to their concerns.

Reflecting Back Reduces Communication Conflicts

Conflicts often arise out of miscommunication. Someone said something that was interpreted a completely different way than the speaker intended. When miscommunications are not cleared up, conflict can result. It is important that your message is clear, and it is equally important that you have assurance that your intended message was received.

A woman showed up at a very popular restaurant with her husband. It was crowded, and there was a long line of people waiting. The woman approached the hostess and asked, "Will it be long?"

The hostess, ignoring her, kept writing in her book. She asked again, "How much of a wait can we expect?"

The woman looked up from her book and said, "About 20 minutes."

A short time later, the announcement came over the loud-speaker: "Willette B. Long, your table is ready."

What you intended to communicate is not always the message that was received. While in some cases this can be humorous, in other circumstances it can cause a great deal of conflict. When you "reflect back" in your communication, you clarify the intended message, or ask for clarification if the message was unclear. Clear and concise communication is a very important aspect of any cohesive relationship.

A judge was interviewing a woman regarding her pending divorce and asked, "What are the grounds for your divorce?"

She replied, "About four acres and a nice little home in the middle of the property with a stream running by."

"No," he said, "I mean what is the foundation of this case?"

"It is made of concrete, brick, and mortar," she responded.

"I mean," he continued, "what are your relations like?"

"I have an aunt and uncle living here in town, as well as my husband's parents."

The judge took a deep breath and asked, "Do you have a real grudge?"

"No," she replied, "we have a two-car carport and have never really needed one."

"Please," he tried again, "is there any infidelity in your marriage?"

"Yes, both my son and daughter have stereo sets. We don't necessarily like the music, but we can't seem to do anything about it."

"Ma'am, does your husband ever beat you up?"

"Yes," she responded, "about twice a week he gets up earlier than I do."

Finally, in frustration, the judge asked, "Lady, why do you want a divorce?"

"Oh, I don't want a divorce," she replied. "I've never wanted a divorce. My husband does. He said he can't communicate with me."

Communication is a two-way street, and it does not require just talking and listening. It requires comprehension and understanding. Reflecting back helps to bridge the gaps of misunderstanding and allows room for clarification.

> *It can be stated with practically no qualification that people in general do not know how to listen. For several years, we have been testing the ability of people to understand and remember what they hear.... These extensive tests led to this general conclusion: Immediately after the average person has listened to someone talk, he remembers only about half of what he has heard— no matter how carefully he thought he was listening. What happens as time passes: Our testing shows...that we tend to forget from one-half to one-third [more] within eight hours.*
>
> —Dr. Ralph G. Nichols,
> *University of Minnesota*

General Tips for Active Listening

There are many useful strategies we can employ when attempting to improve our communication skills. Below are some helpful tips for active listening. Some of the benefits of active listening are also covered below.

✦ *Be aware of your body posture.* Lean slightly forward and face the speaker squarely. Try and maintain an open position without folding your arms. Position yourself an appropriate distance from the speaker.

✦ *Create a nondistracting environment.* Turn off the TV or stereo. Close the door to your office to help prevent interruptions. Attempt to remove any physical barriers like plants, desks, lamps, etc. If you are in a place where you could be disturbed, it might be good to go for a walk and talk.

✦ *Open the door for communication.* You might start with a comment like, "Your face is beaming today," or "You look as if you are not feeling up to par." You can give the person an invitation to continue speaking by saying, "Care to talk about it?" "Please go on," or "I'm interested in what you are saying."

✦ *Short responses encourage sharing.* Often a short response of one to three words will help to open up communication and encourage the speaker to proceed. These responses do not imply either agreement or disagreement with the speaker. However, they do let the speaker know that you are trying to follow the conversation and are interested. Short responses encourage the speaker to continue:

  • "Tell me more."

- "And then what?"
- "What did you do then?"
- "Really?"
- "So?"
- "Sure."
- "I see."
- "Go on."
- "Wow."

Strategic Questions Open Up Conversation

When you ask questions, endeavor to keep them open-ended. This basically means to try and ask questions that cannot be answered with a simple yes or no statement. It is helpful to form your questions in such a way as to encourage the individual to think through his or her answer and assume responsibility for the conclusion. "If you tell off your boss, how do you think that will affect your job with the company?" Reflective questions help the individual evaluate his own motives, ideas, and behavior. It helps the person to clarify his own thinking.

It is important to ask one question at a time and let the speaker answer each one. Do not overload and confuse the person with several questions at the same time. This will help to keep the conversation from getting sidetracked down less important "rabbit trails."

If the speaker asks questions, listen carefully to them. Determine if the person is asking a true question or not. Sometimes people "attack by question."

"You never do what I want to do...do you?" is not a true question. It is really a statement with a question mark at the end.

"Where were you last night?" is probably a statement of judgment and anger. It could be a veiled approach to show disappointment that you were late or did not show up at all.

"What are you doing tomorrow afternoon?" may not be asked because the speaker wants to know your schedule. They may really want to suggest that they need a ride to the shopping center.

"What time is it?" may be asked for another reason than wanting to know the hour and minutes. The speaker might be bored at a party and want to go home.

"How much did you pay?" could be asked because the speaker thinks you paid too much money.

I was at a friend's house one day when his wife said, "Are you going to comb your hair?" I smiled and said, "Why didn't you tell him to hurry up and get ready or we're going to be late?" She responded, "I didn't want to come right out and say that." I said, "But you did." Just because a sentence has a question mark at the end does not mean that it is a true question.

Silence Is Your Friend

Sometimes it is best to just be quiet. Silence gives the other person time to decide whether to talk or not. It gives him time to pull his thoughts together and proceed at his own pace. Do not be afraid of silence. You do not have to fill in the gaps with your talking. Silence often serves as a gentle nudge to go deeper into the conversation. Your eye contact and body posture demonstrate your interest and concern for the speaker. Be silent and observe. Silence can be an effective means of gaining additional information.

Question: "Gail, we are missing a file from the classified file drawer. Do you know anything about it?"

Answer: "I work in a different department."

Silence. Nodding your head up and down and keeping silent may cause Gail to give more information. Most people become nervous when there is silence, especially if they have something to be nervous about.

Answer: "I rarely go over to the classified area."

Silence. Still looking at her.

Answer: "I was only in the classified area one time last week."

Often when a story comes out by bits and pieces, it is because the speaker is trying to hide something. She will often keep talking and watching the questioner until she thinks the listener is convinced.

Listening Can Be Part of the Healing Process

Active listening helps to decrease angry emotions. It helps clarify and clear up misunderstandings. It helps to keep conversation on track. It helps to build relationships. Active listening will help you be a more effective spouse, parent, friend, and leader. It will increase your communication skills. It will help you to learn how to resolve conflict at home, at work, or in the community.

> *One of the first things that every top executive learns is that a very high percentage of his salary goes just to pay him to listen.*

Active Listening Takes Practice

Active listening is not the easiest thing in the world. It takes time, patience, and most of all, practice. If you have a habit of cutting people off, interrupting, or interjecting, it will take some time to break that habit. When you replace the old habit with a new one, you will begin to see a positive pattern of behavior emerge.

If you have a habit of becoming overly defensive or clamming up during conflict, it will take some practice for you to become comfortable with active listening skills and reflecting back as you engage in communication.

Active listening requires that we set aside our pride and stubbornness. It requires that we exercise patience and understanding. This aspect is much easier for the Amiables and the Analyticals than it is for the Drivers or the Expressives. Amiables and Analyticals are natural askers, and they are much more patient by nature. It is much easier for them to listen intently and not cut people off. The challenge for these two social styles is to resist the temptation to either avoid the confrontation or withdraw from it. They must also resist the temptation to be stubborn and clam up. The challenges for the Drivers and Expressives are to listen patiently and not interrupt. They are the natural tellers. They are more than willing to do the confronting, but struggle more with doing the listening. They will share their thoughts and feelings freely, but sitting still and absorbing is more of a challenge.

As you begin to apply these active listening skills, you will notice a reduced level of conflict. You will also notice that conflict does not escalate as quickly, nor does it become as volatile. Active listening says you care, and when people feel like you care, a bridge of trust is built. A strong bridge of trust is much more likely to withstand inevitable conflict than a weak and rickety bridge. Active listening will pave the way to constructive conflict resolution and a more peaceful existence.

Take time out today to pray. Ask God to cultivate a heart to listen intently to other people. Ask the Spirit to remind you to be slow to speak and quick to listen as you work on the fruit of patience and self-control. Let God work in your heart and life as you actively pursue improvement in your listening skills.

28

Dealing with the Response to Confrontation

The end of a matter is better than its beginning,
and patience is better than pride.
—ECCLESIASTES 7:8

—***—

When Jesus confronted the Pharisees about their hypocrisy, He encountered a variety of responses. Anger, resentment, and defensiveness were right at the top. He knew He would be offending them during the confrontation, but He chose to confront the issues anyway.

When you confront someone, there are a variety of responses you can expect. The most common response is defensiveness. If you encounter strong defensiveness, you can be sure that you are not alone. Defensiveness is very predictable. Listed below are seven very common defenses that arise during confrontation:

1. They may refuse to discuss the issue with you. They will not give you the time of day. This is basically an "out-of-sight, out-of-mind" move.

2. They may demonstrate selective hearing and hear only what they want to. They will focus on one of your possible misstatements or incorrect facts. They will make that a major issue so that you will not get to the heart of the matter. This diversion is an "overpower the confronter with words" move.

3. They will let you know that you are not a perfect person. They will bring up your faults to divert the pressure they are feeling. This is an attempt at a "turn the tables on you" move.

4. They give a host of excuses concerning the confrontation. These smoke screens are used to confuse the issue. They will endeavor to convince you that their excuses are valid, and that you need to change your mind about the issue. This is a "confuse your enemy" move.

5. They will merely reject and not accept any points of the confrontation. This is a "straightforward power-play" move.

6. They will try and triangle other people into the situation. They will attempt to get other people on their side. This is an attempt to put social pressure on the confronter. This is a "power in numbers" move. (The next chapter will address triangling in detail.)

7. They will immediately agree with you. "Yes, you are right. I am wrong." This is an attempt to placate you in the hope that if they will agree with you, that you will back off, and they will not have to change. This is a very "clever, subtle, and deceptive" move.

There are many tactics that people will use when having to face confrontation or conflict. Charts 28-A through 28-C list some conflict-avoidance, competitive, and collaborative tactics that you may actually see someone use when confronted. Collaborative tactics can be used to make the confrontation easier.

Conflict Avoidance Tactics

Simple Denial: Unelaborated statements that deny that a conflict is present

Extended Denial: Denial statements that elaborate on the basis of the denial

Underresponsiveness: Failure to acknowledge or deny the presence of a conflict following a statement or inquiry about the conflict by the partner

Topic Shifting: Statements that terminate discussion of a conflict issue before the discussion has reached a natural culmination

Topic Avoidance: Statements that terminate discussion of a conflict issue before an opinion has been expressed

Abstractness: Abstract principles, generalizations, and hypothetical statements that supplant discussion of concrete individuals and events related to conflict

Semantic Focus: Statements about the meaning of words or the appropriateness of labels that supplant discussion of conflict

Process Focus: Procedural statements that supplant discussion of conflict

Joking: Nonhostile joking that supplants serious discussion of conflict

Ambivalence: Shifting or contradictory statements about the presence of conflict

Pessimism: Pessimistic statements about conflict that minimize the discussion of conflict issues

Published by permission of Transaction, Inc. From *Human Communication Research,* vol. 9, no. 1, pp. 85-86, copyright 1982.

Chart 28-A

Competitive Tactics
Faulting: Statements that directly criticize the personal characteristics of the partner
Rejection: Statements in response to the partner's previous statement that indicate personal antagonism toward the partner as well as disagreement
Hostile Questioning: Directive or leading questions that fault the partner
Hostile Joking: Joking or teasing that faults the partner
Presumptive Attribution: Statements that attribute thoughts, feelings, intentions, or motivations to the partner that the partner does not acknowledge
Avoiding Responsibility: Statements that minimize or deny personal responsibility for conflict
Prescription: Requests, demands, arguments, threats, or other prescriptive statements that seek for a specified change in the partner's behavior in order to resolve the conflict
Violence: Use of force to ensure one's will against the other

Published by permission of Transaction, Inc. From *Human Communication Research*, vol. 9, no. 1, pp. 85-86, copyright 1982.

Chart 28-B

Collaborative Tactics

Description: Nonevaluative statements about observable events related to conflict

Qualification: Statements that explicitly qualify the nature and extent of conflict

Disclosure: Nonevaluative statements about events related to conflict that the partner cannot observe, such as thoughts, feelings, intentions, motivations, and past history

Soliciting Disclosure: Soliciting information from the partner about events related to conflict that one cannot observe

Negative Inquiry: Soliciting complaints about oneself

Empathy or Support: Statements that express understanding, acceptance, or positive regard for the partner (despite acknowledgment of a conflict)

Emphasizing Commonalities: Statements that comment on shared interests, goals, or compatibilities with the partner (despite acknowledgment of a conflict)

Accepting Responsibility: Statements that attribute responsibility for conflicts to self or both parties

Initiating Problem-Solving: Statements that initiate mutual consideration of solutions to conflict

Published by permission of Transaction, Inc. From *Human Communication Research*, vol. 9, no. 1, pp. 85-86, copyright 1982.

Chart 28-C

Whenever any tactic is used to avoid conflict or the confrontation, it is usually done in an effort to avoid taking ownership. Collin confronted Kara about an issue at work. Every time he tried to address the issue, she would use a different tactic to avoid taking ownership. Collin had to continue to bring her back to the issue until she finally took ownership.

"Kara, I need to talk to you. I've noticed that you've been coming in late every day for the past week. I need you to be here on time."

"Well, I keep getting stuck in traffic. It's not my fault." Kara was already defensive.

"Then I need you to leave earlier so you can get here on time," Collin responded.

"Stephanie was late last week and no one made a big deal out of it." Kara offered up her second tactic.

"I'm not talking about Stephanie's behavior. I am talking about yours. I need you to be here on time and stop coming in late." Collin was attempting to bring her back to the issue.

"I have been working really hard! I stayed an extra hour yesterday. Does anyone notice when I do anything right?" Kara continued to deflect ownership of the issue.

"Kara, you're an excellent employee. This has nothing to do with that. This issue is about one area of your current behavior: being late for work. I would rather you got here on time instead of staying late. You're setting an example for other employees, too." Collin could feel his patience being tested.

"You're right," Kara finally relented. "I need to get here on time, and I will make sure I do that. I'm sorry for arguing with you about it. I've just had a tough two weeks."

This type of exchange is very common. People initially get defensive and will attempt to redirect the attention elsewhere instead of taking ownership. With effective confrontation, you must patiently bring the person back to the issue until ownership is taken. Chart 28-D shows how a high level of defensiveness makes it difficult for someone to take ownership. As time elapses and defensiveness drops, the chances of someone owning the problem will increase. Successful confrontation and resolution takes a tremendous amount of patience.

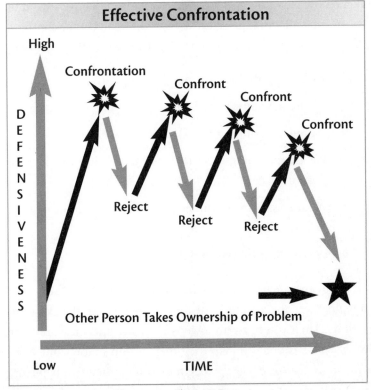

Chart 28-D

There will be situations during this process where emotions will run high, and the person being confronted may get upset. He may begin raising his voice as he becomes more defensive. He may also move to a very offensive role in an effort to avoid taking ownership.

It is always best to attempt to keep the discussions at a moderate level. The increase of pitch, tonal quality, and volume often causes conflict to escalate. The most ideal plan is to "speak softly and turn away wrath." But this is not always possible.

In the cases where volume and emotion run high, we sometimes need to exercise what is called "tone-scaling." The technique of tone-scaling attempts to keep conflict from escalating out of control.

As the other party's voice goes up, our voice may need to parallel theirs. This raising of voice does not mean that we are out of control and attempting to start an outright fight. On the contrary, the raising of our voice is done to let the other party know that:

✦ We are not afraid of them.

✦ We are not going to be bullied by them.

✦ We are not going to back down from them.

✦ We are not going to let their negative behavior continue unaddressed.

✦ We are not going to run from the conflict and the matters to be discussed.

✦ We are there to deal with the issue.

In tone-scaling, you rise to the other person's level of tone and remain there for a time until he becomes aware that you are serious. Then you begin to lower your voice and measure your words. This is done to help the other person follow your lead. Hopefully, his voice will also begin to lower. When that happens, more significant discussion and resolution can occur.

If that does not happen, then you need to be alert to the nearest exit. In all seriousness, tone-scaling is a very effective method of meeting a highly emotional person. It addresses where the person is in his or her feeling level. It helps to move the individual to a point where more meaningful conversation can occur. Chart 28-E provides a visual depiction of what tone-scaling looks like.

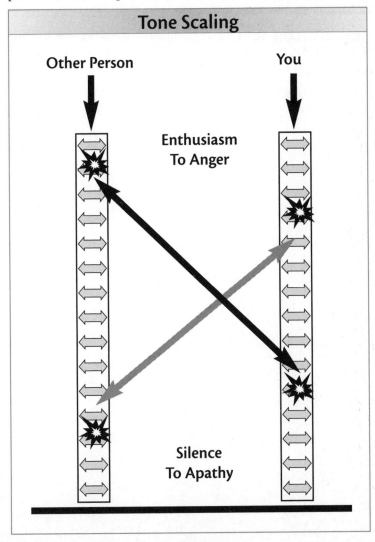

Chart 28-E

Whether dealing with the public, coworkers, family, or friends, confrontation will always be a challenge. People will not always respond as you expect them to. Your buttons may get pushed, and *you* may not react as you would like to. Learning how to deal with confrontation and conflict will help facilitate more cohesive relationships in your life.

If you have the luxury of confronting a fellow believer, offer to start the meeting with prayer. When both hearts are submitted to the will of Christ, you stand a much higher chance of making positive progress.

Before responding to an angry or defensive person that you have confronted, consider taking time out for prayer. Allow God to prepare your heart and give you the right words to say to resolve the issue.

29

When You Are Confronted

Do not be quickly provoked in your spirit,
for anger resides in the lap of fools.
—ECCLESIASTES 6:9

I am sure that you have heard the comment, "You can dish it out, but you can't take it." Well, there is more to effective conflict resolution than just confronting people. What happens when confrontation is served in your direction? What happens when the shoe is on the other foot? How do you react to being confronted? Do you have a thin skin? Do you become angry? Do you become critical? Do you feel threatened? Do you respond like a martyr because you have been picked on? Do you rise up and attack? Is your pride hurt that someone could see you as a problem? Is it hard for you to accept criticism? Is it difficult for your ego to believe that you could be part of the problem? Are you willing to change your behavior? Are you willing to grow?

When you are confronted or verbally attacked, your response is very important. It is a good idea to plan ahead and be prepared in the event that you become the person who is the focus of a confrontation.

What to Do When You Are Confronted

1. *Do not respond immediately to the confrontation.* Take a deep breath and count to ten as you slowly let the air out. This will help to relax you and give you a brief moment to gather your thoughts. This is extremely important if you begin to feel yourself getting angry. Ask God to give you wisdom and patience as you address this confrontation.

2. *Do not raise your voice.* Speak softly and slowly, and measure your words deliberately. If the conflict escalates and the other party proceeds to verbally attack you, tone-scaling may become necessary (see chapter 28).

3. *Thank the confronter for his or her thoughts and feelings.* Let the person know that the complaint is important to you and that you have heard. Thank the individual for having the courage to make the confrontation and taking the time to do it.

4. *Ask for the real issues.* Before you begin to deal with the complaint, ask the confronter, "Are there any other issues you would like to share with me?" This gives the confronter the opportunity to get everything off his chest. Sometimes the complaint is not the real issue. Often the confronter has the real or deeper issue "waiting in the wings" to be shared with you.

   The confronter may "test the water" to see how you will respond before he tells you what he really wants to say. You may have to ask, "Is there anything else?" several times before the entire matter comes to the surface. Do not try and respond to the original complaint until you feel that all the cards are on the table. Otherwise, you may find that you have been set up for an even stronger attack.

5. *Watch body language and listen to tone.* As the confronter is talking with you, observe his body language and tonal quality, along with the verbal message. This will help you to gauge the depth of the confronter's emotions and the strength of the underlying convictions. Remember, you need all the information you can get before you respond.

6. *Seek clarification.* Listen carefully to what the complaint and concerns are. Along the way, ask questions and seek clarification. This will help you keep your own emotions in control and will clear up misunderstanding. As you listen and ask questions, you will convey that you value the confronter as a person and that his ideas are important to you. Sometimes people just want to be heard. You might ask the confronter, "When did you first begin to feel that way?" Or you might ask, "What did I do to give you that impression?"

7. *Watch your own body language.* Be alert to your own body language. What is your eye contact like? Do you find yourself looking away from the confronter, or directly at him? Do not demonstrate your anger or frustration with frowns, sighs, or disagreeing looks. Your body language could escalate the problem. Try and think about your role in the conflict. What have you done to contribute to the misunderstanding or disagreement?

8. *Reflect back what you heard.* Before you respond to the accusations or complaint, rephrase and play back the complaint to the confronter. You might say, "Let me see if I

have heard you correctly." After you have reflected back the complaint, ask, "Have I accurately understood what you have shared with me?" Don't forget to remain silent after each question. Let the confronter respond. Even if there is a long pause, it will help clear up any misunderstanding.

The reframing of the attack or the issue helps to defuse anger and hostility. It gives the confronter a graceful way to stay in the communication game and cooperate toward resolution. Remember, part of conflict resolution is a training process for everyone involved. How you treat others will serve as a model and train other people how to treat you and the other people in their lives.

9. *Watch for unfair confrontations.* Keep in mind that some people do not play fair. They may stay in an attack mode. They may attempt to change the subject. They may confuse the issues by discussing other matters and minor details. Some people only want to throw up their anger and "barf out" all of their hostility. They have no thought or desire for resolution. These people may be wrapped up in anger, rigidity, and intolerance. They may be dealing with fear, paranoia, or some emotional impairment.

In these cases you may have to stop talking about the issues and talk about the process of what is going on. The confronter's dirty tricks and unproductive presentation may need to be exposed for what it is. We can only hope that when the light of truth comes on, the person's method of dealing with issues and his behavior will modify. But that is not always the case. You could be rejected. The only thing you can do is attempt to be open, honest, and firm.

This is all part of the risk-taking involved in conflict management.

10. *Ask for resolution solutions.* Ask the confronter what he would like to see changed. How would he like the matter resolved? You must find out what the other person wants. It is foolish to attempt to resolve the issue until you know all the variables. It is only then that you can say that you agree with the complaint and concerns, or that you will accept part of what he says or wants, or that the answer will have to be no and you are in complete disagreement.

After you employ all of the steps above, you can respond. You will have your emotions under control. You have given yourself some time to clarify and think through the issue. You will be able to determine just how important this issue is. You will be able to more effectively solve the conflict.

Peg Pickering, in her book entitled *How to Manage Conflict,* suggests what is called the ACES approach to conflict.

A—**Assess** the situation.
C—**Clarify** the issues.
E—**Evaluate** alternative approaches.
S—**Solve** the problem.

This approach can certainly be used when you are the one being confronted. Take time to truly assess the situation. Once you have done that, you can clarify the issues and evaluate the alternative approaches. Then you will be in a position to offer potential solutions to the problem. Learning to accept and handle confrontation with wisdom and grace is a lifelong process. As you continue to learn and grow, you will begin to witness some positive changes in your life when it comes to conflict resolution.

When You Are Confronted About Someone Else

What do you do when someone comes to you and wants to vent about someone else? Do you feel like you are being asked to take sides? What if you are friends with both people? How do you prevent yourself from getting sucked into the conflict? One of the most helpful, yet least-used concepts in dealing with annoying people is recognizing the theory of triangling. This concept was developed by a family counselor named Murray Bowen, M.D., in the 1950s.

Dr. Bowen suggested that the smallest form of society consists of two people. If these two people each have a good self-image and a healthy working relationship with each other, there is harmony. What happens when one or both do not have a good self-image or healthy working relationship with each other? There is frustration, tension, and disharmony. This disharmony can lead to arguments, fights, and separation. In some cases it leads to death, which is a permanent cutting-off of the relationship.

> *If we all told what we know of one another, there would not be four friends in the world.*
>
> —Blaise Pascal

In the process of counseling families, Dr. Bowen noticed that families of origin develop "triangles." These triangles are formed when there is disharmony between two of the family members. The individual who feels tension mounting and emotional disharmony to the greatest degree will invariably triangle a third party. A triangle is the smallest stable social relationship.

For example, let's say that a husband and wife are having marital difficulties. The wife might feel the most emotionally disturbed about the disharmony in the marriage. As a result, she could triangle a close friend by venting her frustrations and pouring her energies into that particular relationship. This triangling helps the wife take the focus off the problems with her husband and focus energy on someone else. The result is that the marriage is temporarily stabilized, even if the marital problems are not resolved. The person who feels the most tension needs to vent that tension. The wife might even choose to get involved with someone other than her husband.

Of course, the most ideal thing would be for the husband and wife to resolve the conflict between them. But alas, this is not always done. For some reason, we would rather talk to other people about our problems than personally face the annoying person in our life. Why do you think this is?

Let's further illustrate this concept. Let's suppose that Party A and Party B have a relationship with each other. They may be married. They may be a child and a parent. They might be fellow workers. They could be a boss and an employee or a policeman and a speeder. I think you get the idea. Then some conflict comes between them. Chart 29-A shows the beginning of conflict between two parties.

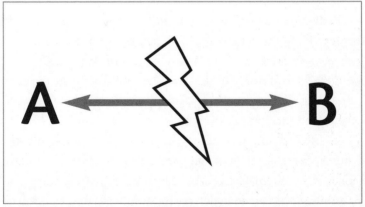

Chart 29-A

Let's say that Party A feels the most discomfort and tension in the relationship. Because of this tension, Party A will triangle a third party. This is where Party C comes into the picture. Chart 29-B shows how Party C forms the triangle.

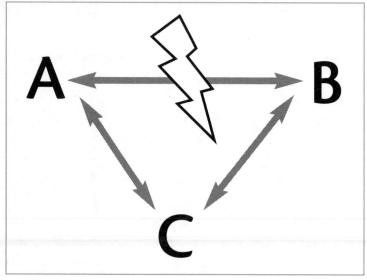

Chart 29-B

Party C has some form of relationship with both parties A and B. Since Party A is feeling the most tension, he begins to unload his frustrations about Party B into the ears of Party C. This may be in the form of storytelling or gossip. It could be under the guise of needing advice and counsel. It might even be as a warning to Party C to watch out for Party B.

In any case, the more Party A unloads his complaints, the better he feels. He might feel good because unloading releases tension. Or, he might feel good because he shared his anger and resentment and helped to destroy the reputation of the person he dislikes. Revenge does taste sweet for the moment. The more Party C listens and agrees with Party A, the closer it draws them together. The closer they are together, the farther it pushes Party B away. Chart 29-C shows how Party B gets pushed away as Party A and Party C talk about party B.

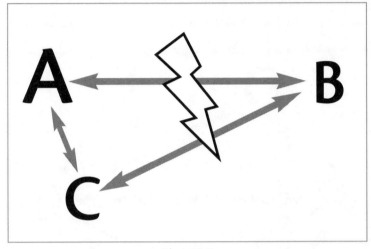

Chart 29-C

This type of triangling happens all the time. If fact, I would be willing to guess that you will be triangled in some form this very week. It might be at home, at work, at church, or in some social gathering. Triangling happens so often that we fail to recognize it for what it is. Triangles are almost automatic and need very little intellectual awareness.

Let's take this a step farther. If the tension is great enough, Party A may not be satisfied with just talking to Party C. This person may feel a need to get more people involved. He may want to build a coalition to force his will or opinions on people with whom he disagrees. Party A may begin to develop a complex network or series of three-person relationships. This development of smaller triangles may be done openly, such as in a rally of some type. However, most of the time it is done covertly at the water fountain, during coffee breaks, over lunch, or at social gatherings. The mainstay for triangling is usually gossip or storytelling. It is a situation where the "understanding ones" get together and talk about those who are not present to defend themselves. Chart 29-D shows the complex web that is often woven through triangling.

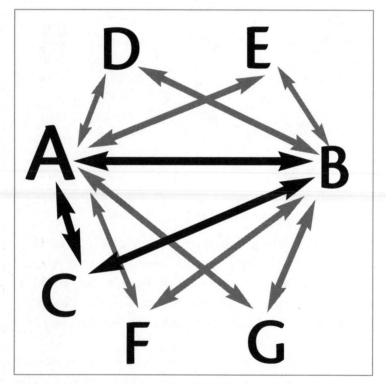

Chart 29-D

Most triangling causes more disharmonies. It generates more hurt feelings and creates dissension among people. It causes friends, relatives, and employees to choose sides against each other. Often, triangling is used as a form of manipulation. It is an accepted method of talking against people like bosses, teachers, ministers, relatives, or close family members.

Have you ever been triangled? Have you been sucked into the whirlpool of hostility before you could swim away? Have you been personally hurt by the annoying people in your life by the use of triangling? Or let's get a little more personal: Have you triangled people and shared your bitterness and anger about other people? Have you been the instigator of hurt?

You see, everyone has played a role in triangling. It is a fact of life. It is part of the human experience. However, it is possible to lessen the negative effects of this powerful social tool.

The first step is to develop awareness about triangling. This requires controlling our spoken words and developing emotional objectivity. It means growing up. The more alert you are to triangling, the more it will lose its power over you.

Do not allow yourself to get sucked into gossip. The Bible offers many warnings against gossip, including, "A perverse man stirs up dissension, and a gossip separates close friends" (Proverbs 16:28). Gossip is like a cancer that spreads through relationships and slowly kills friendships.

> I am more deadly than the screaming shell from the howitzer. I win without killing. I tear down homes, break hearts, and wreck lives. I travel on the wings of the wind. No innocence is strong enough to intimidate me, no purity pure enough to daunt me. I have no regard for truth, no respect for justice, no mercy for the defenseless. My victims are as numerous as the sands of the sea, and often as innocent. I never forget and seldom forgive. My name is Gossip.
>
> —MORGAN BLAKE

When Someone Tries to Triangle You

✦ Do not let your emotions run away with the information handed you. Stay calm and search for truth.

✦ Do not be forced to choose sides. Try and remain untriangled. This is done by objective observation. Learn to see the seriousness of the situation and balance it with the humorousness of the situation. If you are Party C, try to keep the proper emotional distance. Remember that problems between Party A and Party B will automatically resolve themselves if they can get the assistance of an objective third party. Try and bring the two parties together to talk it out, and do not take no for an answer. Meaningful emotional contact without becoming emotionally overinvolved is the key.

> *If you want to change attitudes, start with a change in behavior.*
>
> —WILLIAM GLASSER

✦ Do not accept defeat. If you can help to resolve or modify the conflict in the central triangle, then the other network of smaller triangles will probably resolve itself. The smaller triangles are feeding off the basic first triangle problem. King Solomon said, "Drive out the mocker, and out goes strife; quarrels and insults are ended" (Proverbs 22:10).

✦ Do not forget the importance of a person-to-person relationship. Strive to help others and yourself remember to talk *to* people instead of talking *about* people.

Whether you are confronted, or someone confronts you about someone else, it can be an uncomfortable situation. Many people would rather chew tin foil than have to deal with confrontation. Other people seem to thrive on confrontation. Regardless, someone ends up feeling uncomfortable.

By employing many of the tools and techniques in this chapter, you can equip yourself to adequately cope with the annoying people who confront you. Just remember: Confrontation and conflict are normal elements of life and can actually help you grow. Continue to pray that the Spirit of God will guide your heart in dealing with confrontations.

30

The Influence of Power in Conflict

Do nothing out of selfish ambition or vain conceit,
but in humility consider others better than yourselves.
—PHILIPPIANS 2:3

There is usually some form of power struggle in conflict situations. The power issues can be subtle and underground, or they can be very overt and straightforward. There are many catch phrases that describe the concept of power in human interaction.

- ✦ "There is a real power play going on in our organization."
- ✦ "She is a high-powered person."
- ✦ "He is a control freak."
- ✦ "She is the power behind the throne."
- ✦ "The boss is just being bullheaded."
- ✦ "My supervisor likes to throw her authority around."
- ✦ "That group just bulldozed over us."
- ✦ "I don't appreciate their strong-arm tactics."

Your position in a conflict situation will often determine the outcome. The central factor in most conflicts involves power and control. In chart 30-A, Party A has 50 percent of the power and/or control, and Party B has 50 percent. In this situation, both parties have pretty equal footing.

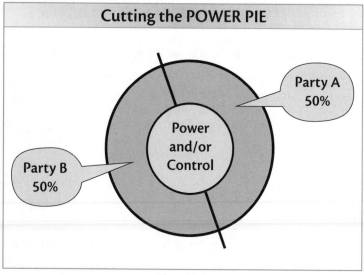

Chart 30-A

In chart 30-B, Party A has 70 percent of the power and/or control, and Party B has only 30 percent. In this case, Party B stands a pretty low chance of determining or dictating the outcome of the conflict.

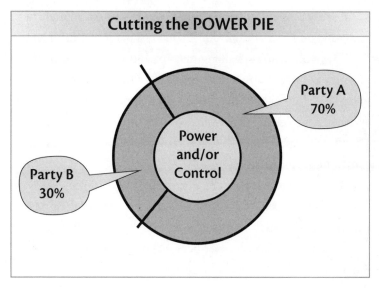

Chart 30-B

Sometimes the power pie is very unbalanced. Some people use their positions of power and authority to cut the power pie nearly 100 percent in their favor. For example, a supervisor in an organization may use the position of authority and power to control conflict and its outcome. If someone approaches this person with a potential conflict, the supervisor merely remind that person about who owns the largest piece of the power pie. "I'm your supervisor, so this is how it's going to be. If you don't like it, I suggest you find somewhere else to work." In this case, the power pie might be cut 99 percent to 1 percent.

In other situations, a person may use his position to positively influence people and empower them to maintain a positive level of control. In spite of his position of authority, he may cut the power pie more evenly and respond differently. "Let's sit down and talk about some viable solutions to this conflict."

In some cases, a disproportionate power pie is absolutely necessary in conflict. For example, if you are a parent and you have a three-year-old who is challenging your authority and is ready to run into the street, you will not have time to argue about who is in control. You will cut that power pie 100 percent in your favor and take complete control of the conflict situation. Your position of authority and power in that scenario will determine the outcome of the conflict.

In organizations, you are not dealing with three-year-olds (though it may seem like it at times), and you are not their parent (though it may seem like that, too!). Whether you have to deal with business relationships or personal ones, you will encounter the many different power approaches often used by people throughout the course of their interaction with others. Below are some of the more common uses of power that you will encounter:

1. *Positional Power:* Power can be seen when people are referring to their position. "Now hear this: I'm the Father/ Mother." "I'm the boss." "I'm the pastor of this church." "I'm the teacher." "I'm the government official." "I'm somebody." "I'm in charge."

2. *Expertise Power:* Power can be seen when individuals refer to their expertise. "I've got a college education." "I've been trained in this." "I've read books on this subject." "I've handled many of these situations before."

3. *Seniority Power:* Power can be seen when people refer to their seniority. "I've been doing this job for 15 years." "I've paid my dues." "I've been asked to consult in this area." "I've been promoted to senior team leader." "I didn't fall off the turnip truck last week."

4. *Resource Power:* Power can be seen when the person is in control of resources. "I control the purse strings." "I write the checks in this organization." "I can cut off their supply any time I want."

5. *Affiliation Power:* Power can be seen in networking contacts. "I know the boss." "I know who is in charge." "I have a friend." "I've got a guy that can get us a good deal." "I met the president the other day at lunch."

6. *Personality Power:* Power can be seen in personality. "I just got elected class president." "They invited me to be the master of ceremony." "I was on television last week." "I gave a speech at the club yesterday."

7. *Godfathering Power:* Power can be seen in "godfathering." "Think of all the things I've done for you." "You're fortunate that I was able to get you that job." "Don't worry about paying back that loan right away." "You owe me some respect." The act of helping people can make them dependent or obligated to the helper. It can be a high-power move masked under the guise of helping.

8. *Acting-out Power:* Power can be seen in the display and use of dysfunctional behavior. This can be in the form of yelling, crying, or rebellious actions. They are strong displays of control. The individual uses this acting out to keep people from challenging his position or influence. Everyone becomes afraid of his strange or unpredictable behavior. The tendency is to back off and let the person have his way.

9. *Group Pressure Power:* Power can be seen in using group pressure. The exercise of "the majority rules" or being "democratic" can force the person in disagreement into

conformity and silence. This method can railroad decisions through board or committee meetings. It is especially effective if the confronting individual is not present at the meeting. The person lobbying for his own position can convince the group of a particular plan or decision. Then later the person who is in disagreement is informed that the group made a decision that goes against him. How do you argue against "the group"? This is a subversive technique for utilizing power and control.

10. *Intimacy Power:* Power can be seen in intimacy. "We really have a close relationship." "I just got the latest word about that merger." "I can't believe that you would treat me that way." "We've been friends for so many years."

11. *Intimidation Power:* Power can be seen in intimidation. "Your job may be on the line over this issue." "If you can't get this job accomplished in time, you may not get the promotion." "I think your supervisor may need to know about this."

12. *Silence Power:* Power can be seen in silence. It is a withholding of information. Silence power is keeping people "out of the loop" or in the dark. It can manifest itself by ignoring or not responding to written or verbal questions. Or it might show itself by excessive periods of noncommunication. And then when some communication does take place, the person exercising the silence pretends like nothing is wrong and everything is normal.

The silence can hide in a busy work schedule, which helps to evade contact with the other party. Comments about being overloaded are provided as the excuse. There is mention of conflicts in time and an inability to get together. "I'm really sorry that we haven't been able to touch base. My workload has been so heavy, you know." They are often followed by suggestions and promises of getting together soon.

The silence even continues when the parties get together at home, at work, or in a social setting. There is only small talk. Nothing of personal importance is shared. No issues are introduced or resolved. It is basically a shutting off of relationships. It is simply treating the other party as a nonperson who does not exist. The Amish use "shunning" to control the behavior of those who might "walk to a different drummer" or who display any type of disagreement with the leadership.

Communication silence is the most destructive force in relationships. It is quite common and is used most effectively at home, in business, and in the community. It is often used to force an individual into submission or frustrate him without having to personally confront the person. It is one of the most powerful forms of passive aggressiveness. It can also be used as a form of revenge and a method to hurt someone without coming out into the open. No one will be able to directly accuse the person using this technique, because there are no spoken comments or nonverbal clues. A person can even smile and pretend to be interested, while using this most subtle and powerful form of control.

> *Silence is full of words we never utter.*

13. *Privilege Power:* Power can be seen in withholding privileges. It may be found in the changing of a person's job to a lesser position of influence or responsibility. Privilege

power can be used to deliberately frustrate a person to the point where he gets angry and quits or pulls out of the marriage relationship. Then the person withholding the privileges gets off the hook because he did not leave—it was the other person. "He could have stayed if he really wanted to."

14. *Passive-Aggressive Power:* It can be seen in the use of other forms of passive aggressiveness. This behavior uses techniques like chronic forgetfulness. "Oh, I'm sorry. I just simply forgot." Isn't it strange how we never forget the things we really want to do? Some of the common passive-aggressive behaviors include:

+ *The behavior of chronic lateness.* Of course, there are lots of excuses. And they are all good.

+ *The behavior of chronic illness.* This occurs often when promises have been made and the person does not want to keep them.

+ *The behavior of conflicts in scheduling.* "Oh, I forgot. I scheduled two things at once. I can't be there." Isn't it interesting how the person cancels your appointment and not the other one? Hmmmm.

+ *The behavior of slips of speech.* This often involves unkind words and then apologizing for them. It seems like an accident at first, but it is not long before a pattern emerges.

+ *The behavior of unkind humor.* "Is that your face, or did your neck throw up?" "Is that your head, or did your body blow a bubble?" "Just kidding, you know." Yeah, I do know. "Can't you take a joke?" This is the "double whammy." You get chopped by the joke itself and by the follow-up comment that you have no sense of humor.

✦ *The behavior of evading issues and other people.* This often inconveniences the people who are evaded. Decisions are delayed and communication is stymied.

✦ *The acting out with nonverbal behavior.* This can be seen in the slamming of doors, dropping things, and banging objects. Then, when confronted, the person denies that there is anything wrong. Passive-aggressive behavior (as well as the other uses of power) needs to be confronted. Confrontation can be a painful and difficult process. It can also be a freeing and healing process for both parties if approached properly.

When Abuse of Power Becomes Physical

It is hoped that you will never have to deal with the physical side of conflict and confrontation. As a rule of thumb, when people escalate conflict to the point of physical involvement, they have come to the end of their verbal skills. When they can no longer communicate or get their point across, they lash out physically. They use and abuse power to get their way.

> *The use of power can leave a legacy that negatively affects relationships. It can create the desire to get even.*

The physical conflict is an attempt to control the situation. A striking-out can be an attempt to gain submission. It is a physical way to let the other person know who the boss is, who has the power, and who is in control. A physical display can also be an attempt to get the other party to back off or withdraw. It is not as much an attack as it is a protection device. But, regardless of the motivation, physical violence tends to separate people and escalate conflict.

This is not a book on martial arts. It is not written with the concept of physically protecting you in a conflict situation. It is written to enhance your knowledge and sharpen your skills in verbally dealing with the annoying people in your life. Yet it is important for you to recognize when verbal conflict starts heading toward a physical confrontation.

There are signs or "red flags" before verbal conflict turns into physical conflict. It is important that you recognize them and do not contribute to making things worse:

✦ The tone of voice gets stronger.

✦ The volume of speech gets louder.

✦ The speed of speech increases.

✦ Name-calling and swearing may be present.

✦ Warnings and threats begin to be issued.

✦ Eyes begin to focus and squint.

✦ Arms begin to wave.

✦ Fists begin to clench.

✦ Walking back and forth may be present.

✦ All of someone's body language begins to look threatening.

✦ Objects might be thrown.

✦ The hitting of doors, walls, and other items starts.

✦ There is forward movement, and the space between people narrows.

✦ Territorial space is invaded.

There is a message here: You are about to be assaulted. It might be wise to be alert to these warning signals. To neglect them may bring about wrath.

When you begin to see trouble coming, do not add extra energy to the tornado in front of you. The result may be more devastating than you would like. Remember, most of the murders that occur happen between people who know each other. When you see the red flags listed above:

+ Try not to raise your voice.
+ Try to remain calm and cool.
+ Do not make fun of the other person.
+ Do not call the other person names.
+ Do not begin to accuse him.
+ Do not make warnings and threats back to the individual.
+ Do not begin to taunt or belittle him.
+ Try to remove yourself from the situation. Walk away. Even run away, if necessary. Do everything in your power to deescalate the situation. This is just plain common sense.

It has been said that "absolute power corrupts absolutely." Those who exercise negative power can develop a false sense of worth. They can begin to believe their own press reports. They can begin to design methods and systems to protect the power they have. They can begin to look down on those who have less power. It is also true that absolute powerlessness also corrupts. It forces people into a position where they have nothing else to lose, so they fight back with rebellious intensity. Tyranny in any form creates and fosters revolution. Revolution can take various forms from very aggressive to very passive.

A wise grasshopper once said, "He who decides who has the power, has the power."

When Great Britain ruled India, it was by sheer force. The Indian people were subjugated. Mahatma Gandhi used only nonviolent resistance to challenge the might of the English. He did not have the finances, resources, or desire to use military strength. He only used his strength of character. In the end, who was really the stronger?

Closing Thoughts

Committing a great truth to memory is admirable;
committing it to life is wisdom.
—WILLIAM A. WARD

━━━━

Conflict is an inevitable part of our lives, and that is not all bad. When addressed properly, conflict can cause us to grow. When approached with the right mind-set, conflict can increase the effectiveness of our relationships. Understanding the people we work and live with will only enhance our ability to reduce and resolve conflict constructively.

The strengths of the annoying people in your life can complement your weaknesses, if you will allow them to. Since you are one of those annoying people, your strengths can also serve to complement the weaknesses of other people. We can all learn and grow as a result of the interaction we have with other people.

> *Nine-tenths of wisdom*
> *consists in being wise in time.*
> —THEODORE ROOSEVELT

I enjoy teaching seminars and workshops on these concepts. It still amazes me how positively people respond to this information. It becomes real, alive, and tangible in their lives. They begin to see why certain people rub them the wrong way. They begin to see why they rub others the wrong way. The light comes on, and they realize why they get along so well with certain people but not with other people.

Many people have contacted me months or even years after attending a training session or workshop on conflict prevention and resolution. One individual called to tell me about his experience. I will call him John.

> This stuff really works. It's been nine months since I started applying these concepts, and I can't begin to tell you how incredible the results have been! I've learned to identify the social styles of people I have to deal with, and now I can accurately predict some of their behavior. This gives me the opportunity to adapt my own behavior to get along better.
>
> Additionally, I have been able to positively confront people that I never could before. I had always viewed confrontation as a negative thing that should always be avoided. I have repaired some hard feelings in relationships through positive confrontation. It hasn't gone perfectly with everyone, but what a difference it has made.
>
> I supervise people at work, and I often have to mediate conflict or be the subject of it myself! I have to deal with annoying people every day, and it's been a real challenge. I have been using many of the conflict-resolution tools that you gave us in the workshop, and it's been amazing. I have been able to diffuse a lot of conflict that had tended to completely escalate in the past. This only motivates me to use more of the tools and continue to learn and grow.

I was getting excited just listening to him! I decided to ask him a question. "If you had to explain to someone else why you think this has been working for you, John, what would you say?"

He responded immediately.

> *Wisdom is the reward you get for a lifetime of listening when you'd have preferred to talk.*
>
> —DOUG LARSON

I have no doubt why it's working. It's working because I am applying the principles. At first I found myself reverting to my old habits and ways of dealing with conflict. I found myself giving in to my natural response to conflict, instead of taking the time to really think through the process. I had to go through a period of time where I actually reconditioned my thinking and my habits of behavior. Instead of sweeping everything under the rug, I forced myself into the habit of confronting issues as they came up and confronting people when I needed to.

I had to recondition myself to really look at the four social styles of people and try to understand why they did the things they did or said the things they said. After doing this for a period of time, it started to become a habit. It's been life-changing, to say the least!

It is great to know that these concepts and information can really change the lives of people in a positive direction. I know it is possible, because I have witnessed it. I have heard many other stories like John's and witnessed the outcome of these applied principles. The key element to true success was brought out in John's account of his own experience: consistent application. An old Latin proverb says, "A nail is driven out by another nail; habit is overcome by habit."

If you hope to experience positive results from the concepts contained in this book, you must commit to a process of application. At first old habits may rear their ugly heads and temporarily dictate behavior. The good news is, we can replace an old habit with a new one, and the brain accepts this change immediately.

> *By wisdom a house is built, and through understanding it is established.*
>
> —Proverbs 24:3

While it does take time for the new habit to become second nature, the new habit can still be adopted immediately. As we begin to consistently apply new habits and patterns of behavior, response, and conflict resolution, we will begin to see positive changes on a large scale.

Skill acquisition is a process we must go through before we can see the changes in ourselves and our lives. You have to first be aware that you need the skills. Then you have to become serious about change. Then you need to apply the concepts. You will first become skillful. Then, after enough time, the new skills will become a natural part of the "new you."

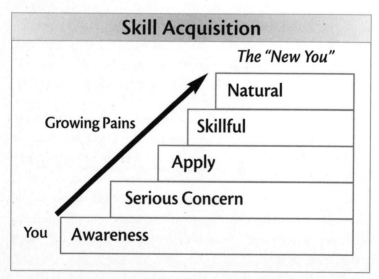

Skill Acquisition

The "New You"

Natural

Skillful

Apply

Serious Concern

Awareness

Growing Pains

You

I encourage you to begin today with some of the principles you have learned in this book. Begin the new patterns of behavior that will create cohesiveness in your personal and professional relationships. Allow yourself the normal temporary setbacks as you grow in your new habits. As you press forward and never give up, may your life become more rewarding and enriching as every day passes. May the Spirit of God transform you as you master the conflict in your life!

> *If you want to change your life, you must*
> *do it immediately and flamboyantly.*
>
> —WILLIAM JAMES
> *American psychologist and philosopher*

Bibliography

Aldag, Ramon J., and Buck, Joseph. *Leadership & Vision.* New York: Lebhar-Friedman Books, 2000.

Alessandra, Anthony J. *Non-Manipulative Selling.* Reston, VA: Reston Publishing Co., 1981.

Augsburger, David. *When Caring Is Not Enough.* Ventura, CA: Regal Books, 1983.

Bolton, Robert, and Bolton, Dorothy G. *Social Style/Management Style.* New York: AMACOM, 1984.

Carson, Robert. *Interaction Concepts of Personality.* Chicago: Aldine Publishing Co., 1969.

Cathcart, J. *The Acorn Principle.* New York: St. Martin's, 1998.

Condon, John C. *Interpersonal Communication.* New York: Macmillan Publishing Co., Inc., 1977.

Cory, Lloyd. *Quotable Quotations.* Wheaton, IL: Victor Books, 1985.

Elgin, Suzette Haden. *The Gentle Art of Verbal Self-Defense.* Englewood Cliffs, NJ: Prentice-Hall, Inc., 1980.

Fast, Julius. *Body Language.* New York: Pocket Books, 1971.

Filley, Alan C. *Interpersonal Conflict Resolution.* Palo Alto, CA: Scott, Foresman and Company, 1975.

Gilbert, Roberta M. *Extraordinary Relationships.* Minneapolis, MN: Chronimed Publishing, 1992.

Hallesby, Ole. *Temperament and the Christian Faith.* Minneapolis, MN: Augsburg Publishing House, 1940.

Hefley, James. *A Dictionary of Illustrations.* Grand Rapids, MI: Zondervan Publishing Co., 1997.

Hendricks, Howard, and Phillips, Bob. *Values and Virtues*. Sisters, OR: Questar Publishers, Inc., 1997.

Hersey, Paul, and Blanchard, Kenneth H. *Management of Organization Behavior*. Englewood Cliffs, NJ: Prentice-Hall, Inc., 1969.

Hocker, Joyce, and Wilmont, William W. *Interpersonal Conflict*. Dubuque, IA: William C. Brown Publishers, 1985.

Jandt, Fred E. *Conflict Resolution Through Communication*. New York: Harper & Row, Publishers, Inc., 1973.

Keirsey, David, and Bates, Marilyn. *Please Understand Me*. Del Mar, CA: Prometheus Nemesis Book Co. Inc., 1984.

Krebs, Richard L. *Creative Conflict*. Minneapolis, MN: Augsburg Publishing House, 1982.

Kreider, Robert S, and Goossen, Rachel Waltner. *When Good People Quarrel*. Scottsdale, PA: Herald Press, 1989.

LaHaye, Beverly. *How to Develop Your Child's Temperament*. Eugene, OR: Harvest House Publishers, 1977.

LaHaye, Tim. *Transformed Temperaments*. Wheaton, IL: Tyndale House Publishers, 1971.

———. *Understanding the Male Temperament*. Old Tappan, NJ: Fleming H. Revell Co., 1977.

———, and Phillips, Bob. *Anger Is a Choice*. Grand Rapids, MI: Zondervan Publishing Co., 1982.

Leman, Kevin. *The Birth Order Book*. Old Tappan, NJ: Fleming H. Revell Co., 1985.

Liberman, David J. *Never Be Lied to Again*. New York: St. Martin's Press, 1998.

Littauer, Florence. *Personality Plus*. Old Tappan, NJ: Fleming H. Revell, Co., 1983.

———. *How to Get Along with Difficult People*. Eugene, OR: Harvest House Publishers, 1984.

Luft, Joseph. *Of Human Interaction*. Palo Alto, CA: Mayfield Publishing Company, 1969.

McKay, Matthew, Davis, Martha, and Fanning, Patrick. *How to Communicate: The Ultimate Guide to Improving Your Personal and Professional Relationships*. New York: MJF Books, 1983.

Mehrabian, Albert. *Silent Messages*. Belmont, CA: Wadsworth Publishing Co., 1971.

Merrill, David W., and Reid, Roger H. *Personal Styles and Effective Performance.* Radnor, PA: Chilton Book Co., 1981.

Myers, Isabel B., and Myers, Peter B. *Gifts Differing.* Palo Alto, CA: Consulting Psychologists Press, Inc., 1980.

Nierenberg, Gerard. *The Art of Negotiating.* New York: Hawthorne Books, Inc., 1968.

Nierenberg, Gerard I., and Calero, Henry H. *How to Read a Person Like a Book.* New York: Pocket Book, 1973.

Pease, Allan. *Signals: How to Use Body Language for Power, Success, and Love.* New York: Bantam Books, 1981.

Peter, Laurence. *Peter's Quotations.* New York: Bantam Books, 1977.

Phillips, Bob. *Controlling Your Emotions Before They Control You.* Eugene, OR: Harvest House Publishers, 1995.

————. *The Delicate Art of Dancing with Porcupines.* Ventura, CA: Regal Books, 1989.

————. *42 Days to Feeling Great.* Eugene, OR: Harvest House Publishers, 2001.

————. *The All-American Quote Book.* Eugene, OR: Harvest House Publishers, 1995.

————. *The Star-Spangled Quote Book.* Eugene, OR: Harvest House Publishers, 1997.

————. *Phillips' Awesome Collection of Quips & Quotes.* Eugene, OR: Harvest House Publishers, 2001.

————. *Phillips' Book of Great Quotes & Funny Sayings.* Eugene, OR: Harvest House Publishers, 1993.

Ruesch, Jurgen. *Disturbed Communication.* New York: W.W. Norton & Company, Inc., 1972.

Scheflen, Albert E., and Scheflen, Alice. *Body Language and Social Order.* Englewood Cliffs, NJ: Prentice-Hall, Inc., 1972.

Selye, Hans. *Stress Without Distress.* New York: Harper and Row Publishers, Inc., 1974.

Solomon, Muriel. *What Do I Say When…A Guidebook for Getting Your Way with People on the Job.* Englewood Cliffs, NJ: Prentice Hall, 1988.

Stowell, Joseph. *Tongue in Check.* Wheaton, IL: Victor Books, 1994.

Turner, D., and Greco, T. *The Personality Compass.* New York: Barnes & Noble, 1999.

Wahlroos, Sven. *Family Communication*. New York: Macmillan Publishing Co., Inc., 1974.

Wainwright, Gordon R. *Body Language*. London, England: Hodder Headline Plc, 1985.

Wakefield, Norman. *Listening*. Waco, TX: Word Books, 1981.

Walters, Richard. *How to Say Hard Things the Easy Way*. Irving, TX: Word Publishing, 1991.

Wright, Norman H. *More Communication Keys for Your Marriage*. Ventura, CA: Regal Books, 1983.

About the Authors

—⟶⟶⟶—

Bob Phillips holds a Ph.D. in counseling and is a licensed marriage and family therapist in the state of California. He is the cofounder of Pointman Leadership Institute. This organization has presented countless seminars on ethics and the importance of character in leadership in over 30 countries.

Bob has written more than 80 books with more than seven million copies sold. His books include *Anger Is a Choice; Over the Hill & On a Roll; Men Are Slobs, Women Are Neat; Great Thoughts and Funny Sayings;* and *Jolly Jokes for Older Folks.*

When not speaking or writing, Bob can be found mountain climbing, cave exploring, motorcycle riding, or enjoying his most important interests: his wife, daughters and sons-in-law, and his three grandsons.

—⟶⟶⟶—

Kimberly Alyn, Ph.D., is an author and international professional public speaker. She is also the CEO of Perfect Presentations, a company dedicated to professional training and speaking services for corporations, small businesses, municipalities, and churches.

Kim is also the author of *Soar with Your Savior, Public Speaking Is Not for Wimps!,* and *101 Leadership Reminders.* Kim's educational and research background include management, psychology, and leadership. She holds a doctorate in organizational management with a specialty in leadership. She is a lifelong learner and thrives on the opportunity to share her quest for knowledge with other people.

When not speaking or writing, Kim enjoys spending time with her family and friends. She lives on the central coast of California and enjoys flying, drawing, and engaging in various outdoor activities.

How to Schedule
One of the Authors
for a Speaking Engagement

KIMBERLY ALYN:
Call 1-800-821-8116
or
log on to:
PerfectPresentations.net

BOB PHILLIPS:
Call 1-559-305-7770

Books on Relationships from Harvest House Publishers

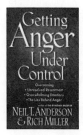

Getting Anger Under Control
Neil T. Anderson & Rich Miller

Whether horrific enough to grab headlines or minor enough to cause arguments with your family and friends, uncontrolled anger steals peace, joy, and trust between you and those you care about. Here you can get clear, biblical methods for keeping your anger in its place.

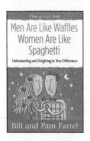

Men Are Like Waffles—Women Are Like Spaghetti
Bill and Pam Farrel

Men keep life elements in separate boxes; women intertwine everything. Providing biblical insights, sound research, and humorous anecdotes, the Farrels explore gender differences and preferences and how they can strengthen your relationship.

Keeping Your Cool...When Your Anger Is Hot!
June Hunt

The fiery emotion of anger often causes us to say and do things we later regret. And try as we might, it's an emotion that's tough to control. How can you prevail? June helps you explore the various causes and kinds of anger and the biblical steps toward resolution and real, lasting change.

When Pleasing Others Is Hurting You
David Hawkins

Christians are called to be servants, caring for the needs of other people. But when you begin to forfeit your God-given calling and identity in an unhealthy desire to please others, you move from servanthood to codependency. How can you get back on track?

How to Get Along with Difficult People
Florence Littauer

Discover unique insights into dealing with the difficult personalities we all encounter at home or work. This updated, expanded edition of a classic provides fresh direction, encouragement, and skills if you need to get along with a difficult person.

Hot Topics for Couples
Steve & Annie Chapman

Based on almost 500 surveys, Steve and Annie Chapman pinpoint communication problems in marriages. They use this information, their own experiences, and biblical principles to help you create a loving partnership with open, satisfying communication.